2450

CIVIL WAR COLLECTOR'S ENCYCLOPEDIA Vol. III

Military Materiel, Both American and Foreign,
Used by the Union and Confederacy

by

Francis A. Lord

Published by
LORD AMERICANA & RESEARCH, INC.
1521 Redwood Drive
West Columbia, S. C. 29169

Copyright © Francis A. Lord 1979
All Rights Reserved
Library of Congress Catalog Card Number: 63-14636
ISBN 0-916492-02

TO

Bill Moore of Baton Rouge, Louisiana

A real expert and
a great friend

FOREWORD

Because of the enthusiastic response to the first two volumes of the *Collector's Encyclopedia,* the author early realized that new data and previously unknown items of the 1861-1865 war **must** be preserved for posterity! Literally hundreds of letters both from home and abroad, have brought in new information. The assistance of these contributors has been substantial in preparation of this book. In several instances they have come up with important variations of items which appeared in the first two volumes of the *Encyclopedia* as, for example, some interesting types of mess kits. Of course, these variations are included in the present volume.

INTRODUCTION

I make no point in praise either to the author or to the contents of this Civil War Encyclopedia; it is my wish to be factual. Dr. Lord needs no 'yes' man to assure him, or any other, that he is presenting a service of revelation — the memorable artifacts in use by the Blue and Gray. What once were the fancies and foibles of conjecture in the contest between the North and the South are now becoming a proud excitement of historical discovery.

> "The bravest men that ever fought
> For this land of ours were boys.
> That boyhood faith may this day renew,
> Till it rivet a friendship chain
> To hold us close and keep us true
> While the last two boys remain."

This poem, written by a newspaper man in dedication to the survivors, both the Blue and the Gray, no longer can be applied to the valiant veterans who gathered for a Regimental Reunion. It can, however, score with triumph "To hold us close and keep us true" — we, the descendants of this heritage. In coordination with the 'leadership' of this Encyclopedia we are finding ourselves important contributors to the continued unearthing of our Civil War history. Yea, in the author's acknowledgements of and to those of us who "have contributed very substantially and unselfishly to this third volume", falls the gist and meaning of this work — its publication, coupled with the contributions of each historian and relic buff, has brought forth a proud excitement of discovery. Too, what we have brought to light further enhances our national heritage, giving us the degrees of eager students who are continually developing greater knowledge that brings forth delightful pleasure of fact. More importantly, perhaps, such knitting together of newly-brought-to-light memorabilia is fostering fast friendships that otherwise may not have been possible. This common ground of our deep love of the War Between — —, has brought about, and will continue to do so, a kinship of one abiding interest; history continues to grow, and friendships become more deeply cemented . . . "To hold us close and keep us true."

There is no need to expostulate on the author's handling of the items described and pictured, the contents speak for themselves. The subjects are many and varied, with no pretense attempted to glorify or romance. The articles are simply and succinctly described, giving due credit to the reader's intelligence of the item presented in a precise way — its meaning, its use, and, in many instances, its proof of soldiers ownership. Webster defines encyclopedia as . . . "General education; a work that contains information on a particular branch of knowledge, usually in articles arranged alphabetically by subject." Ah, then we have such in Dr. Lord's Civil War Collector's Encyclopedia, Volume 3! The contents run the gamut from Adjutant's Knapsack, Confederate, to Writing Kit, Yankee. Little doubt remains as to the item being factual, for manufactures material is described, dimensions are given, "where found" brings proof of battle or campsite use, as well as identification of soldiers ownership so inscribed for posterity. The author freely bows in appreciation of all contributions, giving due credit to all who combed their personal collections to aid in the continued research of Civil War knowledge.

Dr. Lord acknowledges there is "much work to be done", whether it be cleaning materials for uniforms and equipment, Confederate canteens that "are constantly turning up", or mess kits that "continue to intrigue the collector." Indeed so! If this were not true, the battle would be won with no intrigue remaining to continue the delving into fact. This, then, gives us the impetus to search more, to question further, to bring to light. Perhaps the most revealing fact is the realization that this volume, an extended and expanded search of the previous two, does even more to bring together all who express their desire for greater knowledge of this, our American Heritage through destiny.

Mayhap I do, after all, praise Dr. Lord for this presentation. For without his painstaking research, without his patience, durability and understanding of the collector's idiosyncracies, such a compilation of encyclopedic history may never have come to light. What greater knowledge to spur us on!

"Why they fought, why lost, who triumphed, who was wrong, or who was right,
Matters not; They were our brothers, and were not afraid to fight.
Let us form a noble order with sweet freedom for our shrine,
And for each enwreath a token — The Palmetto and the Pine."

In full realization of the historic 'worth' of this Encyclopedia,
I am — Jack Magune

ABOUT THE AUTHOR

Since his retirement as Professor Emeritus in History from the University of South Carolina, the author has concentrated his research on Civil War artifacts. This third volume in the series is the result of his continuing effort to utilize his extensive knowledge of Civil War memorabilia with the enthusiastic support of qualified experts, both here and abroad.

As governor of the Company of Military Historians and Associate Curator of Military History, South Carolina Museum Commission, he maintains close contact with other Civil War experts and museums. This contact is constantly expanding by his frequent appearances as guest speaker to Civil War Round Tables and similar historically oriented groups interested in the 1861-1865 struggle. By means of an extensive correspondence with collectors all over the world as well as his specialized displays of Civil War items at gun shows, Dr. Lord keeps on top of new discoveries in the field of Civil War collecting.

For over thirty years the author has contributed specialized studies on the Civil War to American and foreign journals. In addition, he has written the following:

They Fought for the Union (1960)

Civil War Collector's Encyclopedia, Volume I (1963)

Bands and Drummer Boys of the Civil War (1966)

Civil War Sutlers and Their Wares (1969)

Lincoln's Railroad Man: Herman Haupt (1969)

Uniforms of the Civil War (1970)

Civil War Collector's Encyclopedia, Volume II (1975)

Civil War Collector's Encyclopedia, Volume III (1979)

x

ACKNOWLEDGMENTS

As with the previous two volumes of the *Civil War Collector's Encyclopedia,* this third volume has been made possible by collectors' contributions. The following individuals, genuine enthusiasts in preserving Civil War memorabilia, have contributed very substantially and unselfishly to this third volume. Not only am I personally indebted to their assistance, but present and future collectors as well! Unless otherwise indicated, however, items shown are from the author's collection.

DELMER P. ANDERSON; Santa Maria, California
MARGIE BEARSS; Brandon, Mississippi
ARTHUR LEE BREWER; Durham, North Carolina
W. A. CLARK; New Egypt, New Jersey
ROBERT CORRETTE; Fitzwilliam, New Hampshire
R. V. CROFOOT; Orlando, Florida
ROGER DAVIS; Keokuk, Iowa
TOM S. DICKEY; Atlanta, Georgia
CHARLES EDELMAN; Homeland, California
W. E. ERQUITT; Atlanta, Georgia
MAURICE GARB; Baton Rouge, Louisiana
RODNEY O. GRAGG; Montreat, North Carolina
E. CANTEY HAILE, JR.; Columbia, South Carolina
DAVE HANNAH; Rexburg, Idaho
T. SHERMAN HARDING, III; Orlando, Florida
DAVE HOLDER; West Sussex, England
BILL HOWARD; Delmar, New York
JOHN HUGHES; Battle Creek, Michigan
FRANK A. HUNTSMAN; Hutchinson, Kansas
ROBERT E. JONES; Benton, Arkansas
LON WILLIAM KEIM; Coralville, Iowa
WILLIAM LANGLOIS; San Francisco, California
J. W. LEECH; Grand Junction, Colorado
RICHARD LUCAS; Rodeo, California
TOM MacDONALD; Eustis, Maine
H. MICHAEL MADAUS; Milwaukee, Wisconsin
JACK MAGUNE; Worcester, Massachusetts
CRAIG MARGISON; Riverside, California
JOHN MARGREITER; St. Louis, Missouri
JOHN A. MARKS; Memphis, Tennessee
KEN MATTERN; Wayne, Pennsylvania
JAMES M. McCAFFREY; Houston, Texas

WILLIAM C. McKENNA; Westmont, New Jersey
BILL MOORE; Baton Rouge, Louisiana
DAVID M. MORROW; Woodbridge, Virginia
CLYDE E. NOBLE; Athens, Georgia
SEWARD R. OSBORNE, JR.; Olivebridge, New York
RONN PALM; Monroeville, Pennsylvania
JEFF PEFFER; Etters, Pennsylvania
GERALD F. SAUER; Santa Rosa, California
VERNON SCOONE; Baltimore, Maryland
LOUIS G. STOCKHO: Vero Beach, Florida
A. L. TAFEL; Newark, Delaware
MIKE WOSHNER; Pittsburgh, Pennsylvania

Special thanks to RON TUNISON of Elmhurst, New York for the cover jacket.

CIVIL WAR COLLECTOR'S ENCYCLOPEDIA ADDITIONS AND CORRECTIONS TO VOLUME TWO

Since publication of Volume II of *Collector's Encyclopedia,* the following additions and contributions have been submitted by the readers. The author is sincerely appreciative of these contributions.

William A. Clark; New Egypt, New Jersey. **SUBJECT:** Solingen Military Products (pp. 178-179). Kirschbaum & Bremsley used the symbol "D" as shown on page 179 (a knight's helmet) under the firm name of: C. R. KIRSCHBAUM-SOLINGEN.

Dr. E. Cantey Haile, Jr.; Columbia, South Carolina. **SUBJECT:** Bleeder (p. 9). Doctor Haile identifies this definitely to be a surgeon's "bleeder". This was a device to initiate bleeding by a spring-triggered series of small blades which penetrated the skin about ⅛ of an inch.

Richard Lucas; Rodeo, California. **SUBJECT:** Identity of Federal cavalryman on page 29. He is SUMNER A HALWAY, Co. "H", 1st Maine Cavalry. Halway (Sept. 28, 1839-Feb. 28, 1919) enlisted September 27, 1861 and was discharged for disability November 20, 1863.

Craig Margison; Riverside, California. **SUBJECT:** OLI buckle (p. 17). Cites two authorities who identify this buckle as OGLETHORPE LIGHT INFANTRY and **not** OHIO LIGHT INFANTRY.

ADJUTANT'S KNAPSACK (C.S.) 1

ADJUTANT'S KNAPSACK (C.S.): A very rare Confederate adjutant's knapsack. The frame is of pine wood, covered with black canvas on oil cloth material. The straps are of cotton.

Dimensions: 15 inches tall, 15 inches wide, 4¼ inches deep. Equipped with drawers of pine wood.

Markings: On one drawer, written in pencil: LT. W. E. CAMPBELL
Co. "F" 8th S.C.I.
Bratton's Brig.
Field's Division
Longstreet's Corps
  A.N.V.
General R. E. Lee Commanding
8th April 1865

2 ADJUTANT'S KNAPSACK (C.S.)

ALABAMA CUTLASS (C.S.) 3

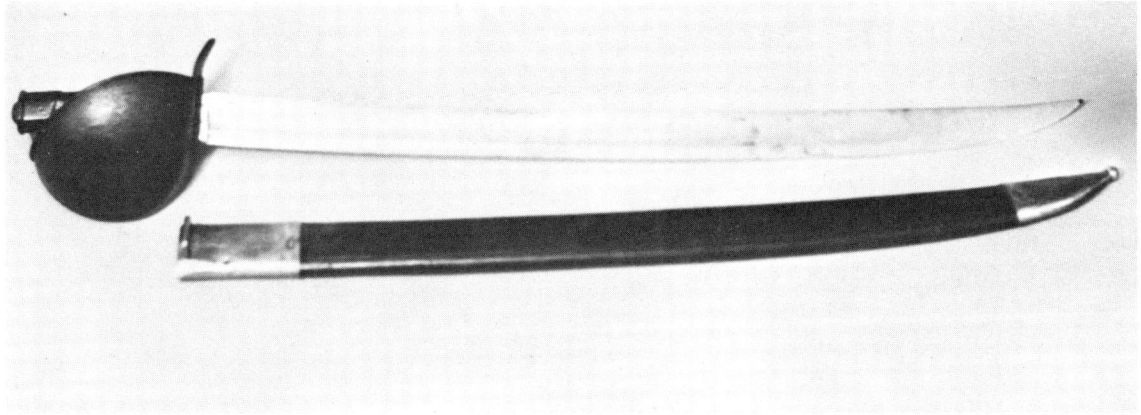

ALABAMA CUTLASS (C.S.): An undated cutlass taken off the Confederate ship **Alabama** in 1864. From the collection of the Commandant, Washington Navy Yard, Washington, D.C.

Dimensions: Length overall — 33 inches; Length of blade 26½ inches; Width of blade 1⅜ inches. Black painted hand guard; black leather scabbard with brass furniture.

4 ANDERSON TROOP IDENTIFICATION DISC

ANDERSON TROOP IDENTIFICATION DISC: A rare "dog tag" worn by CALEB B. KIMBER of the Anderson Troop of Philadelphia (15th Pennsylvania Cavalry). Caleb Kimber was a member of Co. "B". [T. SHERMAN HARDING, III; Orlando, Florida]

ARTILLERY BRIDLE (U.S.) 5

ARTILLERY BRIDLE (U.S.): Made of heavy black leather, measuring 25½ inches from top of headstall to bottom of bit. The brass rosettes on each side of the blinders are 1½ inches in diameter and are decorated with **U.S.** in black letters. This bridle was used by a New York unit during the War.

6 ARTILLERY GUN SIGHTS

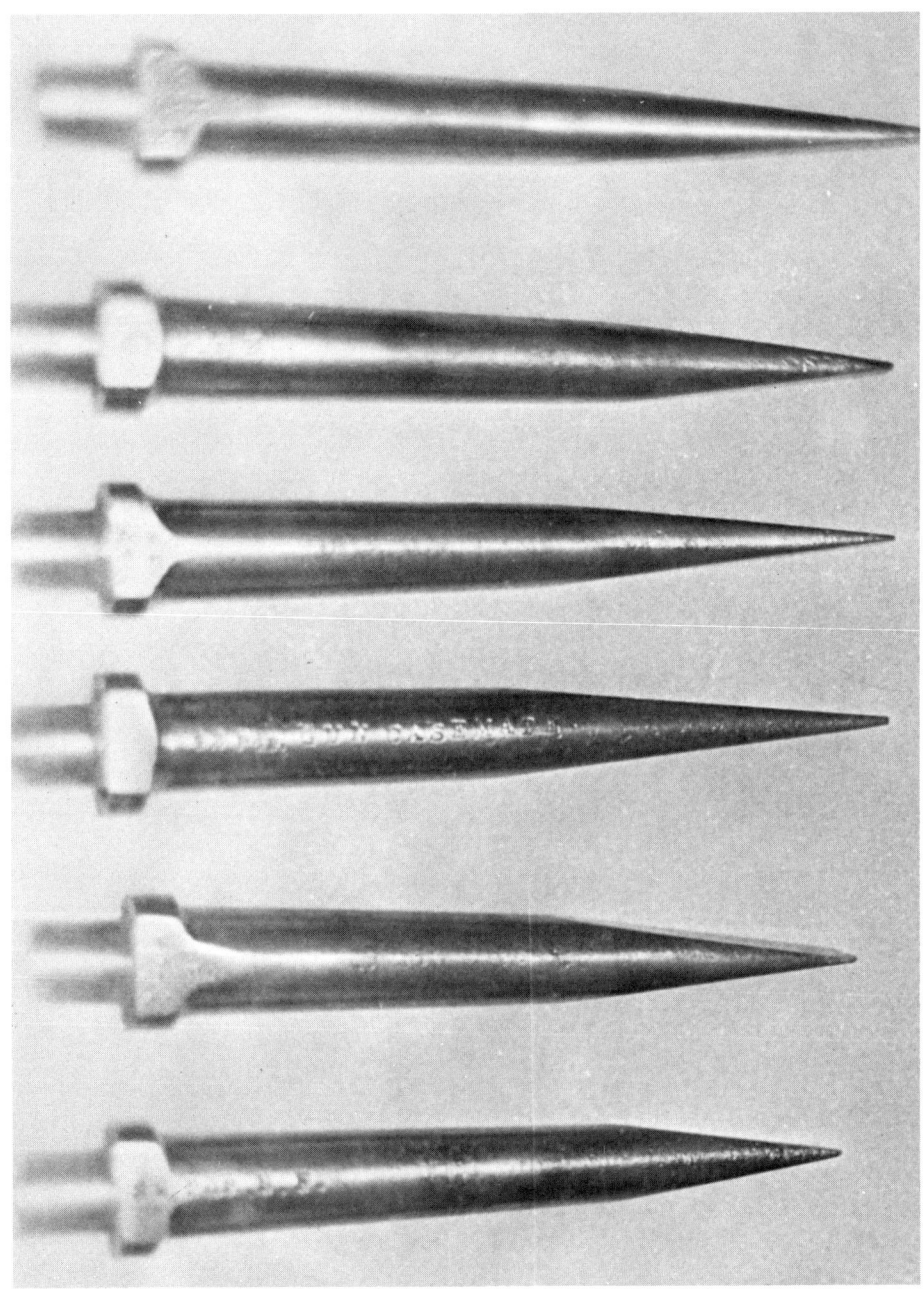

ARTILLERY GUN SIGHTS: Shown here are examples of artillery gun sights from the collection of W. E. ERQUITT of Atlanta, Georgia. These sights are for cannon ranging from howitzers up to large Parrotts and comprise only half of ERQUITT'S fine collection. Each sight is marked for its particular gun type.

AXE HEADS 7

AXE HEADS: Most relic seekers have found axe heads on battlefields and campsites. Shown here are eight examples. Reading left to right:

Top Row:

From C.S. breastworks at Port Hudson. **Dimensions:** 8 inches long with a 4⅞ inch blade.

From the Whitmarsh Battery, Georgia, 1862. **Dimensions:** 6¼ inches long with a 4½ inch blade. **Marked:** 8.

Bottom Row:

From the battlefield of Spotsylvania. **Dimensions:** 7⅝ inches long with a 4¼ inch blade.

From the camp of the U.S. 2nd Army Corps at Falmouth. **Dimensions:** 7¼ inches long with a 5 inch blade.

8 AXE HEADS

From Sherman's campsite at Edward's Station, Mississippi. **Dimensions:** 7½ inches long with a 5 inch blade.

From Stafford Heights, Fredericksburg. **Dimensions:** 7 inches long with a 5½ inch blade.

From camp of the 16th Arkansas Infantry at Port Hudson. **Dimensions:** 6¾ inches long with a 4¼ inch blade.

From Jackson's headquarters at the Yerby House, Fredericksburg. **Dimensions:** 8 inches long with a 5 inch blade.

AXE SHEATHS 9

AXE SHEATHS: Certainly axe sheaths are among the rarest of Civil War items. The two shown here are both definitely of the Civil War era; the sheath with the flap is of black leather — 9½ inches long, 4½ inches wide. **Markings:** Aug. 2, 1864.

The longer sheath is brown leather and originally had a strap and belt loops. It is 9⅝ inches long at the top, 10 inches long at the bottom and is 6 inches wide. **Markings:** Axe Sling, January 1863.

10 BARRACKS LAMPS

BARRACKS LAMPS: These two brass lamps were found in a collection of supplies for a U.S. barracks during the Civil War. They are typical of the non-military lamps purchased by the Federal Government for use at the permanent installations at the staging depots behind the front.

BARRACKS LAMPS   11

12 BARRACKS MATCH BOXES

BARRACKS MATCH BOXES: Barracks were generally heated by wood stoves and the match boxes shown here were nailed or screwed to the barracks' wall. These are both made of cast iron. The bottoms of each are ribbed for striking matches. Lids are decorated in an attractive manner as shown in the photograph.

Dimensions of Each: 4 inches long, 2½ inches wide, 1⅛ inches deep.

Markings: Match box on the left: SELF CLOSING FOR MATCHES
Patented Dec. 20, 1861
H. W. & Co.
New Haven

Match box on the right: Picture of a dog and
PAT'D Jan. 21, 1862

BARRACKS MATCH BOXES 13

Porcelain Match Box: Dimensions: 4½ inches long, 2½ inches wide, 1¼ inches deep. Inside of cover is ribbed to permit striking of matches. **Markings:** Crossed flags on front and back. On top there is a replica of U.S. fractional currency — 25 cents, March 3, 1863.

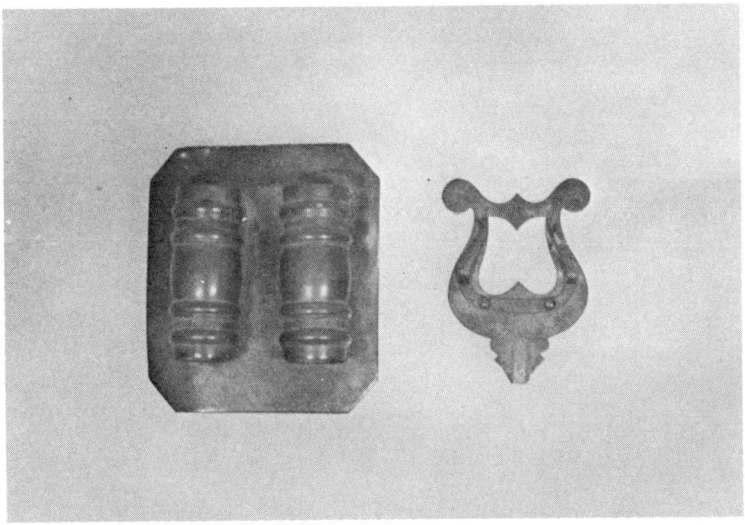

BATTLEFIELD MUSICAL INSTRUMENT ITEMS: As is well known the Civil War regiments had their own bands as well as company fifers, buglers, and drummers. Shown here are various items recovered from camp sites and battlefields. The drum stick holder came from a Rhode Island unit's picket post 4 miles out of Harper's Ferry. The music sheet holder is from the battlefield of Fisher's Hill, Virginia. The horn

14 BATTLEFIELD MUSICAL INSTRUMENT

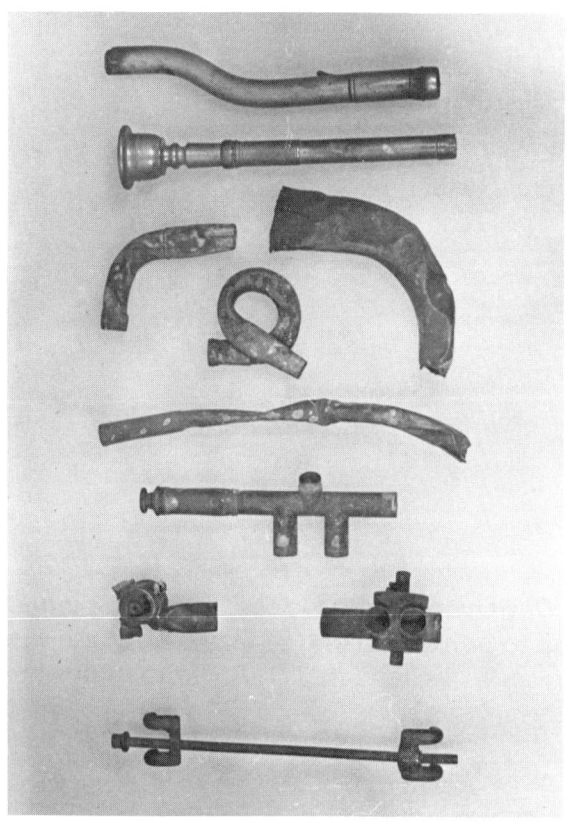

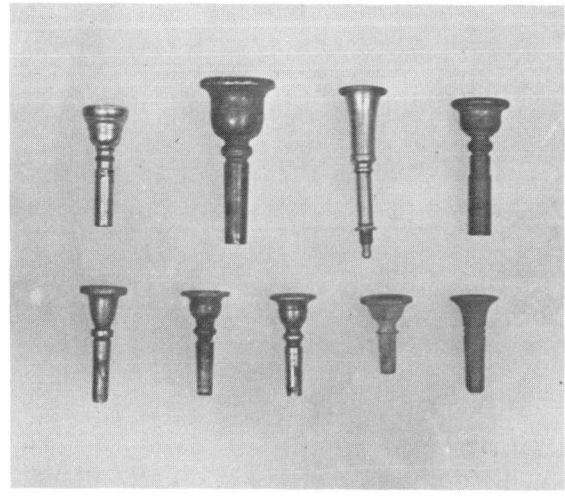

fragments are from Antietam while the mouth pieces were found on various battlefields and camp sites.

BAYONET SCABBARD TIPS 15

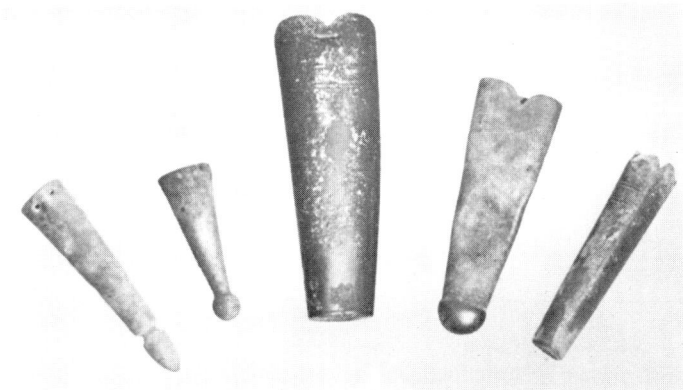

BAYONET SCABBARD TIPS: The leather bayonet scabbards were tipped with brass, pewter, steel or iron. Among the beginning collectors there is some confusion as to identification of these scabbard tips when recovered from the ground. The five shown here may be of assistance in recognizing the basic types. All came from battlefields.

Left to right:

Brass. Springfield rifle musket bayonet scabbard, 3 inches long, from the **Wilderness.**

Iron. Austrian musket bayonet scabbard, 2⅛ inches long from Champion's Hill.

Iron. Enfield short rifle bayonet scabbard, 3⅛ inches long, from Spotsylvania.

Brass. Unknown rifle or musket, sword bayonet scabbard, 3½ inches long, from LaGrange, Tennessee.

Iron. Enfield rifle musket bayonet scabbard, 4 inches long, from Vicksburg.

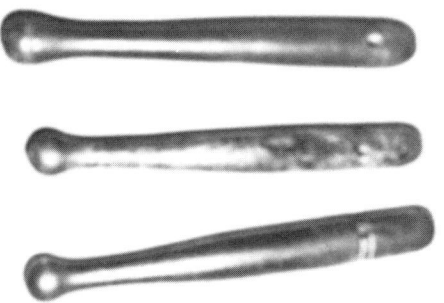

BELAYING PINS: These were used on board naval vessels to secure the ropes. (They were also useful in cracking skulls in attempts at mutiny!) Blackened with age, these pins appear to be of very stout oak. They vary in size from 12¾ to 13⅛ inches in length and about 1½ inches in diameter. No markings.

16 BINOCULARS

BINOCULARS: A typical and interesting pair of binoculars used at Fort Fisher, North Carolina.

Markings: L'ingenieur Chevallier Opt.
Inside the top corner in ink: Gen. Terry used this glass in his reconnaissance of Fort Fisher.

Capt. G. F. Towle
4th New Hampshire
Jan. 14, 1865

BINOCULARS 17

(Towle was captain of Co. "F" 4th N.H. Inf. He enlisted September 11, 1861 and was mustered out August 23, 1865 as major of his regiment.)

18 BLACKING FOR SHOES

BLACKING FOR SHOES: The Federal troops, especially in the East, were "spit and polish" soldiers. Shoes and boots had to be kept polished. Shoe blacking for this purpose was purchased from sutlers. The blacking came in tin cans with paper or stamped labels. Shown here are examples of both types. The paper label specimen was made by Mason of 138 and 140 North Front Street in Philadelphia. This can is of thin tin, 3½ inches in diameter. The other can was dug up at Falmouth, Virginia and is marked: Army & Navy
     made by
F. Brown & Co.
Boston
BLACKING

BOX CLAMP 19

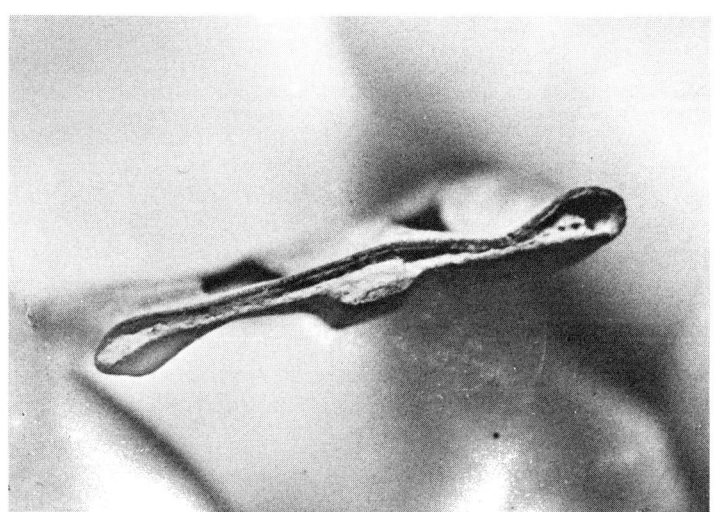

BOX CLAMP: This is a small, highly oxidized metal object found outside of Gettysburg in an area of troop movements just behind the Confederate lines. This object appears to have been used to clamp a metal band, such as a packing band around a crate or box of supplies. It is non-ferrous, probably brass, and measures 1¼ inches long, by ¾ inch wide, by 1/16 inch thick. It is double thickness of sheet metal. In making this object, two parallel ½" long by 1/16-1/8" wide slots were cut in a piece of

20 BOX CLAMP

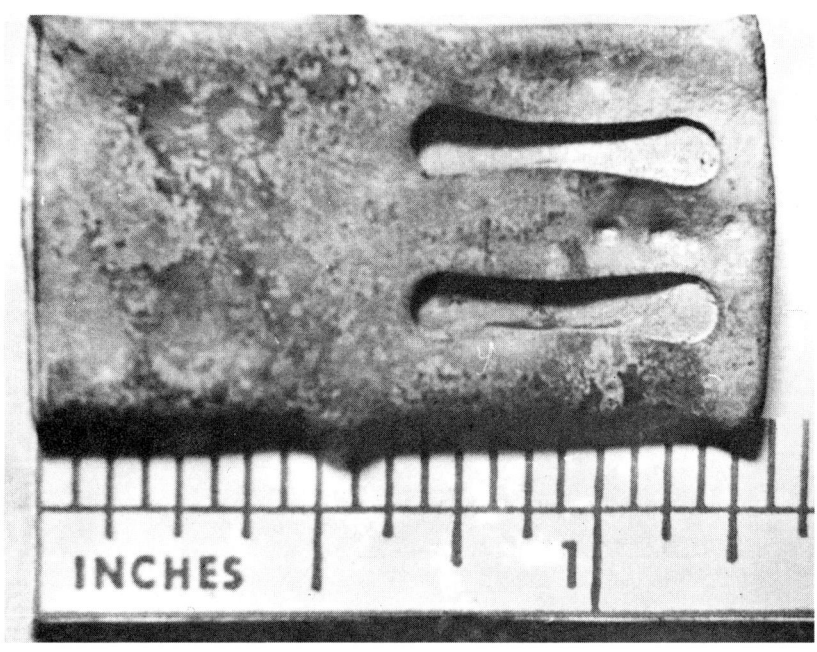

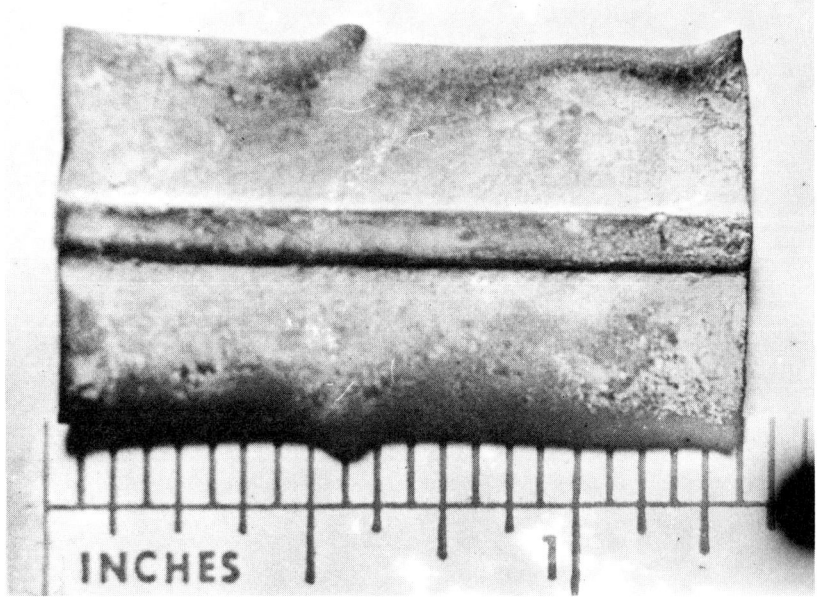

sheet metal; it was then folded, the ends joined in a center seam behind the slots, flattened, and possibly crimped. It appears as though it was used to clamp a metal ½" wide band which was passed through the slots; the center and edge of this "clamp" were punched several times with a pointed punch as if to lock such a band in place.
[JEFF PEFFER; Etters, Pennsylvania]

BRANDING IRON 21

BRANDING IRON: A Federal branding iron picked up years ago on the battlefield of Shiloh, Tennessee. It is 18¼ inches long and the branding surface itself is 2½ inches wide. [TOM S. DICKEY; Atlanta, Georgia]

22 "BREAK-AWAY" STIRRUPS AND SPUR

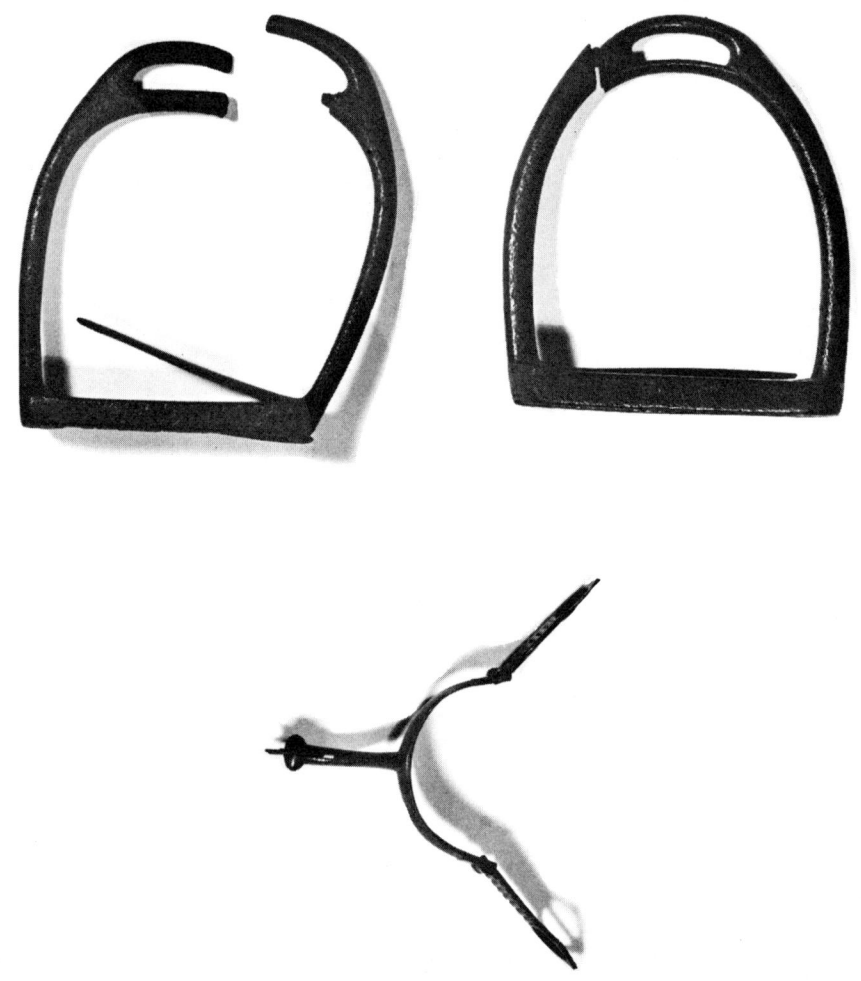

"BREAK-AWAY" STIRRUPS AND SPUR: Shown here are two variations of "break-away" stirrups, probably dating from 1861, although no information on their manufacture is known. They are not marked. The one partly opened, is from the big cavalry battle at BRANDY STATION, Virginia, June 9, 1863. The other is from CULPEPER, Virginia. These stirrups were so constructed as to open out and release the foot of the rider, thus preventing him from being dragged to his death. The spur is hinged, permitting easy attachment or detachment from the boot. [Stirrups — Collection of JACK MAGUNE]

CAMP CHAIR 23

CAMP CHAIR: Camp chairs appear fairly frequently in collections and in contemporary war photographs. This one has especial interest, not only because its original owner is known but its maker as well. Made of oak with strong carpet-like material for the seat, the chair is marked as follows:

Trade Mark: B. J. Harrison
New York.

And painted on the chair are the initials H. M. G. which stand for HARLOW M. GUILD who was First Lieutenant of Co. B., 113th Pennsylvania Infantry.

Shown also is a somewhat plainer type also used in the war. It is from the collection of ARTHUR LEE BREWER, JR.; Durham, North Carolina.

24 CAMP CHAIR

CAMP CHAIR 25

26 CAMP CHEST

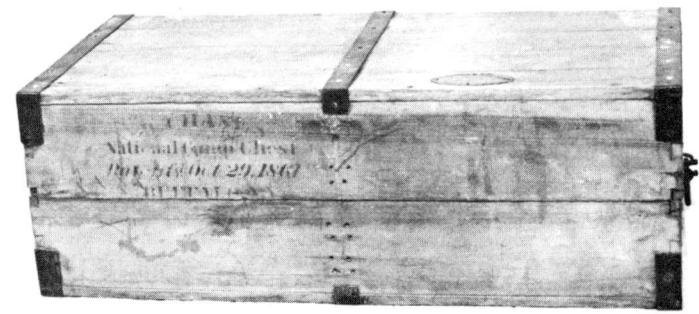

CAMP CHEST: Made of stout oak with iron bands and handles.

Dimensions: 30¼ inches long, 14 inches wide and 10 inches deep.

Markings: On an oval brass plate (3¾ inches long and 2⅛ inches wide at widest point): W. CHASE
　　　　　PATENTED
　　　　　Oct. 29th 1861
　　　　　BUFFALO, N.Y.

　Also, stencilled on front:　W. CHASE
　　　　　NATIONAL CAMP CHEST
　　　　　PAT. Oct. 29, 1861
　　　　　BUFFALO, N.Y.

CARBINE AMMUNITION BOX 27

CARBINE AMMUNITION BOX: As one would expect, all wooden ammunition boxes of the Civil War are extremely rare. Most of the wooden boxes were burned by soldiers to keep warm. (Naturally, only after removal of contents!) The box shown here is of pine wood, 17 inches long, 10½ inches wide, and 6¼ inches deep.

Markings: CARTRIDGES
SHARPS CARBINE
CAL. 52   1864

And — on one side: WATERVLIET
ARSENAL.

This box was picked up from the battlefield of Winchester, Virginia (September 19, 1864).

28 CARVED TOY CANNON

CARVED TOY CANNON: These lead cannons were found in camp sites; they were made by soldiers attempting to pass some time. The larger, is 5½ inches long, was dug at New Salem Church battlefield in front of Kennesaw Mountain. The Minie ball which the maker intended as the cannon's projectile can be seen at the end of the barrel and the vent hole can be seen near the other end.

The smaller cannon is 4 inches long and was found in a U.S. camp before Spanish Fort, Alabama. It blew up at the vent. After the soldiers made these novel toys they could not resist trying to fire them. They just did not realize that black powder explodes too violently to be contained by a lead tube. [TOM S. DICKEY; Atlanta, Georgia]

CAVALRY BELL 29

CAVALRY BELL: A horse bell used when horses were hobbled at night. The bell would be on one horse so the horses could be easily located when needed. This bell belonged to David M. Anderson, 4th Iowa Cavalry, grandfather of its present owner, Colonel Delmer P. Anderson, U.S. Army — Retired, Santa Maria, California. The 4th Iowa Cavalry served at Vicksburg and in the Georgia campaign.

The bell is rather elaborately decorated. The shield and sunburst design is repeated three times on the bell's circumference.

Dimensions: 4¼ inches tall with a diameter at bottom of 4¾ inches.

Made of good quality bronze. A sharp blow causes it to audibly ring for more than 30 seconds. [COLONEL DELMER P. ANDERSON; Santa Maria, California]

30 CAVALRY BELL

Also shown here is a cast brass bell from the camp of the 2nd Iowa Cavalry at LaGrange, Tennessee. This bell is 4½ inches tall with diameters from 5½ inches to 3⅝ inches. Since the handle, pin, and ferrule have been restored, we do not know the original carrying attachment. [JOHN A. MARKS; Memphis, Tennessee]

CAVALRY BUGLE 31

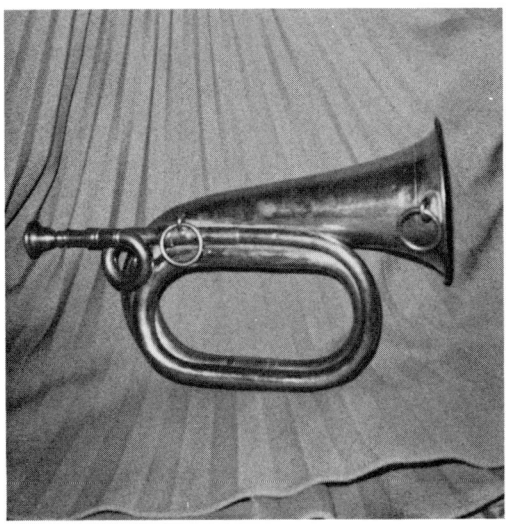

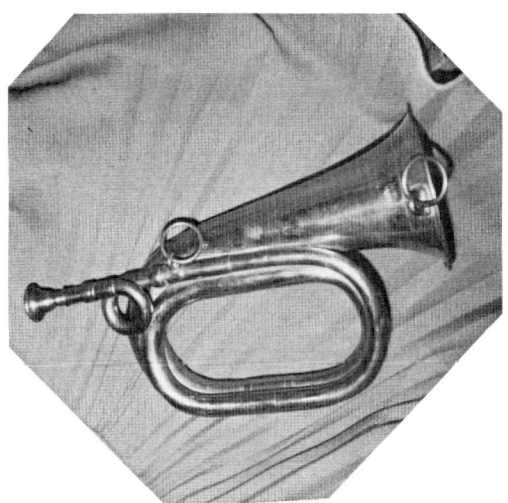

CAVALRY BUGLE: As collectors well know, Civil War cavalry bugles varied significantly in appearance and size. Many bugles were 10¼ inches long with a bell diameter of 3¾ inches. Shown here is a fine specimen of a variation on the more common types; this one is 11½ inches long with a bell diameter of 4½ inches. [DR. CLYDE E. NOBEL; Athens, Georgia]

32 CAVALRY HORSE BRUSH

CAVALRY HORSE BRUSH: Most Federal cavalry horse brushes were made under contract for general army use with no specific State designation. Here is an interesting exception — a brush made for Maine cavalry unit use. The hand strap is stamped: **WARRANTED ALL BRISTLES 90.** On the brush is embossed the seal of the State of Maine. This horse brush was used in the war by Lieutenant FRANK W. PRAY, Co. "I" 1st Maine Cavalry. [T. SHERMAN HARDING, II; Orlando, Florida]

CAVALRY TAR BUCKET, C.S. 33

CAVALRY TAR BUCKET, C.S.: Improvised from a tin coffee boiler, 5 inches tall and 4¾ inches in diameter. Some tar is still inside! Used by a C.S. cavalryman from Petersburg to care for his horse's hooves. **No markings.**

34 CAVALRYMAN'S WALLET

CAVALRYMAN'S WALLET: Brown leather, 6¾ inches long and 3⅜ inches wide. Contains locks of hair from Father and Mother of LLEWELLYN T. WING, Co. "I" 2nd Maine Cavalry (shown in photograph).

Markings: Soldier's name and home address.

Note: The picture of the cavalryman shown here is through the courtesy of RONN PALM who has the original **CARTE DE VISITE** from which the picture was made.

CAVALRYMAN'S 35

36 CHAIN FOR WHIFFLE TREE

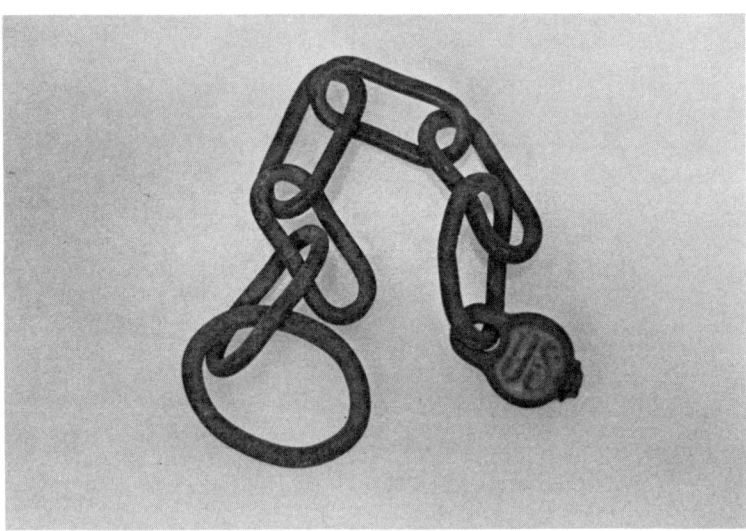

CHAIN FOR WHIFFLE TREE: Section of a whiffle tree chain used by artillery. Each link is about 2½ inches long. At one end is a circular piece of metal 1⅜ inches in diameter with the letters **U.S.** on each side. From the Battle of Winchester, Virginia, September 19, 1864.

CHEVAUX-de-FRISE: Oak tip of a Chevaux-de-frise defense at **PETERSBURG.** The section shown here is about ¾ inch in diameter. Chevaux-de-frise were logs traversed with wooden poles pointed at the end. Normally these poles were 5-6 feet long and were used to defend a position against cavalry and infantry attack. In the Civil War they were used extensively in front of intrenched positions, e.g. the siege of Petersburg.

CLEANING MATERIAL 37

CLEANING MATERIAL: There is still much research to be done on the cleaning materials used by the soldiers to keep their uniforms and equipment in good shape. Depicted here is the container of some type of cleaning material produced and sold by JOHONNOT & SAUNDERS of 21 Dock Square, Boston. Not shown is a round piece of beeswax, 1 inch in diameter imported from England for sale by sutlers. This beeswax cake was used to polish uniform buttons. The cake is marked: FRANCIS
ULLATHORN
LONDON

The top of the beeswax cake is decorated with the British crown.

38 CLIMBING IRON (C.S. TELEGRAPHER)

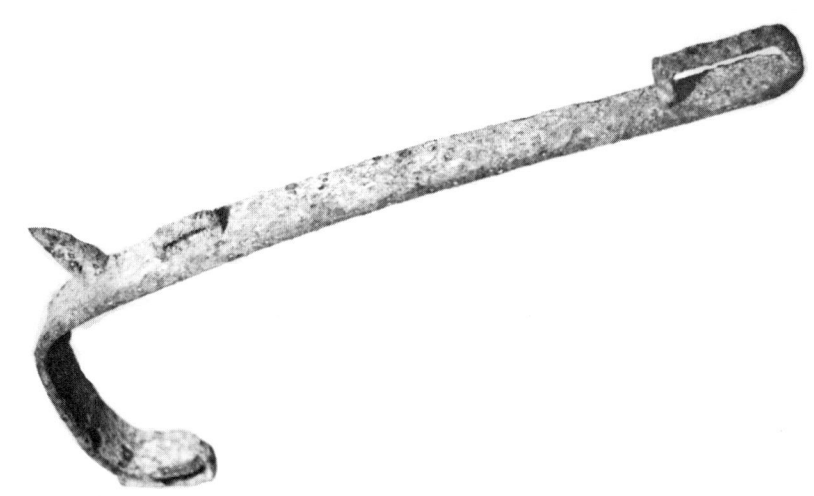

CLIMBING IRON (C.S. TELEGRAPHER): Metal climbing or leg iron used by telegraphers to climb telegraph poles in the field. The iron is 13½ inches long, 1¼ inches wide, with a pointed "spike" 1½ inches in length. Found in a C.S. camp at Front Royal, Virginia. No markings. [JACK MAGUNE; Worcester, Massachusetts]

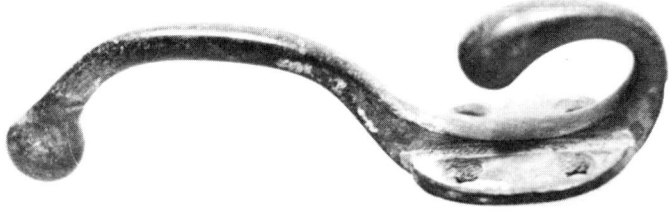

COAT HOOK FOR BARRACKS: Interior furnishings for Civil War barracks are extremely rare. Shown here is a coat hook recovered from the site of a Confederate barracks at Fort Fisher, North Carolina. The hook is of heavy brass, 5½ inches long, with 4 holes for screwing on the wall. [RODNEY O. GRAGG; Montreat, North Carolina]

CONFEDERATE BOWIE KNIVES

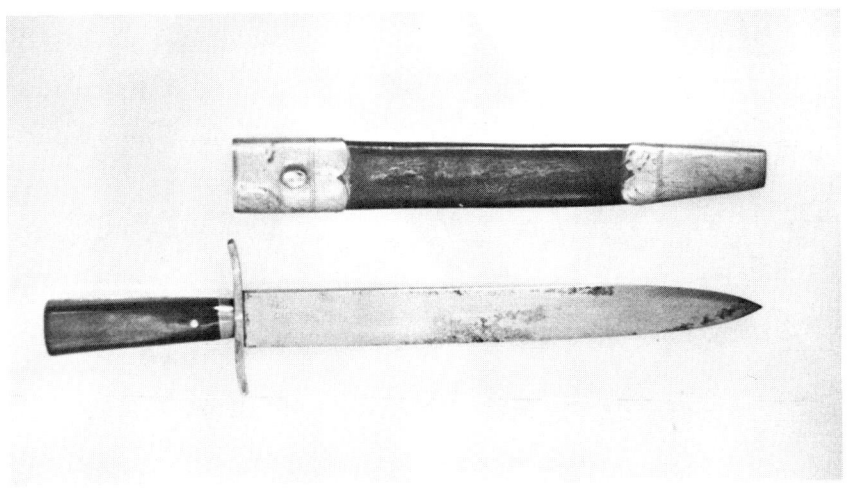

CONFEDERATE BOWIE KNIVES: Confederate bowie knives continue to interest collectors, especially because of the great variations in style and dimensions. Shown here are an individual knife and a grouping — both from separate collections. The individual C.S. bowie knife is 17 inches long with a blade 12⅜ inches in length and 1⅜ inches wide. It has a brass guard and wood grip. The blade is marked on one side:
CONFEDERATE
SELF DEFENDER.

On the other side: YEOMAN (?)
                        CVTL - - - - -
                        C.S. (?).

It has a leather scabbard with brass furniture.

The grouping (next page) consists of 4 knives as follows:

TOP:

   Knife with a 16½ inch blade. Possibly made from a Georgia pike. Leather scabbard.

   Knife 22½ inches long, oak grip — massive D guard.

   Knife 13½ inches long. Iron D guard. Has a 2 inch wide blade with a clip point with false edge. Dug up at Alexandria, Virginia [grip is a possible replacement].

   Knife 14 inches long, with a rosewood grip and wooden scabbard.

[ARTHUR LEE BREWER, JR.; Durham, North Carolina]

40 CONFEDERATE BOWIE KNIVES

CONFEDERATE CANNON SIGHTS 41

CONFEDERATE CANNON SIGHTS: Shown here are two cannon sights for British Blakeley cannon shipped to the Confederacy via the blockade runners.

The sight marked **NO. 628** is a brass muzzle sight which came off the 30-pounder Blakeley recovered from the Roanoke River in North Carolina at the site of Fort Branch.

The ring-shaped sight is a breech sight for the 3.5 Blakeley gun recovered from the sunken blockade runner GEORGIANA. [TOM S. DICKEY; Atlanta, Georgia]

42　CONFEDERATE CANNON SIGHTS

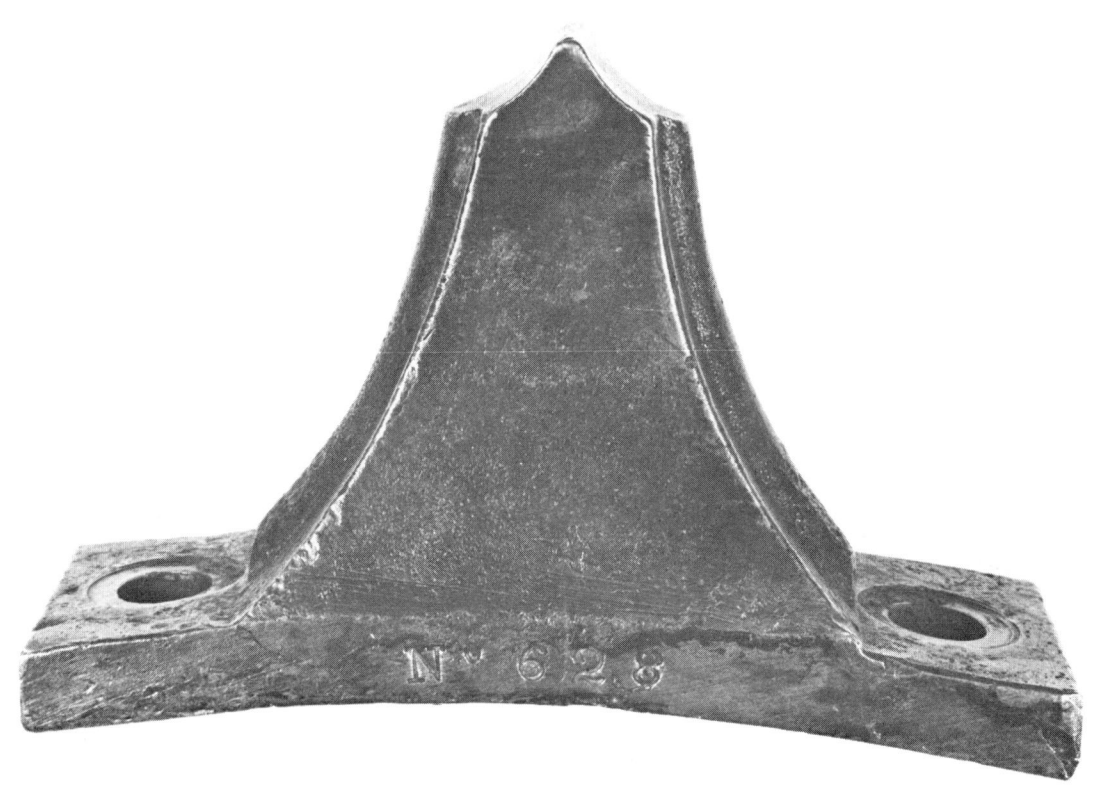

CONFEDERATE CANTEENS   43

CONFEDERATE CANTEENS: Various types of C.S. canteens are constantly turning up. Depicted is a large copper canteen which is 8⅛ inches in diameter and 2⅛ inches deep at the center. This canteen holds exactly 3 pints. The markings are clearly shown in the photographs. **S & K** refers to **SCHNITZLER AND KIRSCHBAUM**, a German exporter of military supplies during the Civil War.

The two tin canteens shown here are probably typical of many used by Johnny Reb. The diameters of both are the same — 6⅛ inches. But one is 2 inches deep while the other is only 1⅝ inches. There are no markings on either specimen.

44 CONFEDERATE CANTEENS

CONFEDERATE CANTEENS 45

46 CONFEDERATE CAP BOX

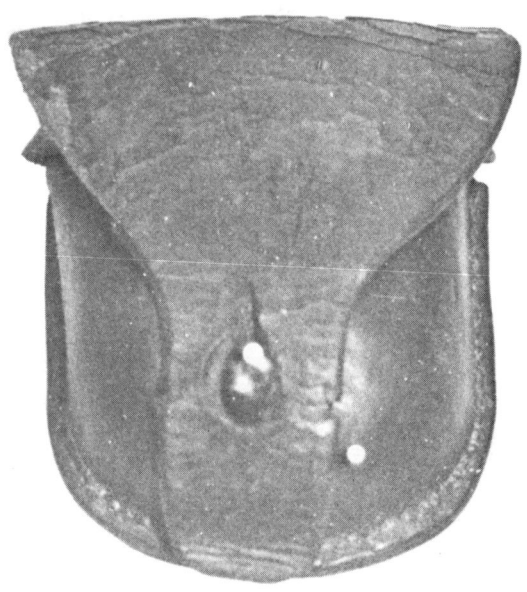

CONFEDERATE CAP BOX: Made of black leather 3¾ inches tall and 3 inches wide. This has an unusual inside covering flap, much different from the U.S. cap boxes. There are two leather loops in back for attachment to the waist belt. No markings. From Fort Macon, North Carolina taken by a Federal soldier after the fort's surrender on April 23, 1862.

CONFEDERATE FLAG 47

Unit Designation:

Color:

Field	Canton	Stars
three horizontal bars, red, white, and red, bound on three sides with 1¼" deep gold fringe; motto "FOR LIBERTY WE STRIVE" in gold, 2" high Roman letters in center bar.	dark blue, 40½" on the staff by 29" on the fly with 2" high white Roman letters "CSA" in its center.	ten (10), white, 5 pointed stars, each 6½" in dia., six set in a circle, 15½" in diameter and one in each corner.

Material: silk field and lettering   silk canton & letters   silk

Method of attachment to the staff not determined

61" (exclusive of fringe)

20¼"

20¼"

20½"

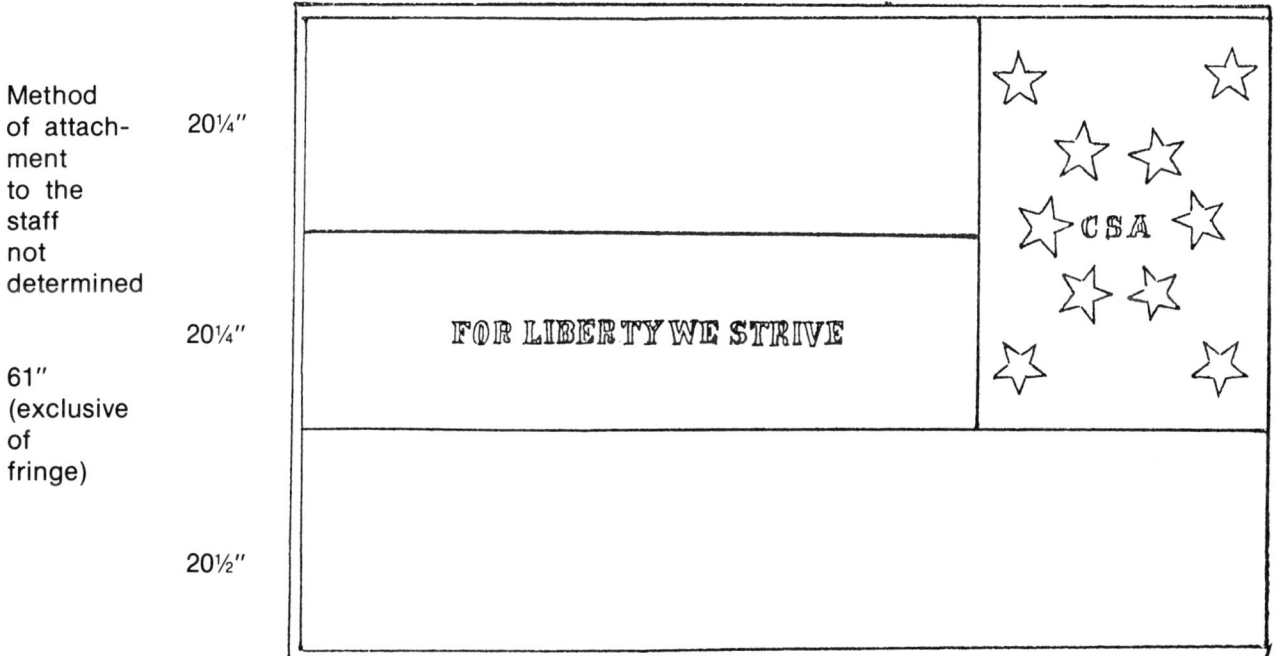

98" (exclusive of fringe)

Note: Motto is sewn to reverse bar only.

CONFEDERATE FLAG: A recently acquired C.S. flag is depicted in the sketch shown here. This flag came from a G.A.R. post and was one of the first Confederate flags captured in Virginia during the war. The capturing unit was very probably from Pennsylvania. **Very** substantial assistance in tracing this flag's history has been rendered by H. MICHAEL MADAUS, Assistant Curator of History, Milwaukee Public Museum. Mr. Madaus is a highly recognized authority on C.S. flags. "Mike" Madaus has authored some extremely fine research studies on Confederate flags.

48 CONFEDERATE COFFEE POT

CONFEDERATE COFFEE POT: Very rare — and used early in the war — because it is made of heavy copper. There are no markings on this coffee pot which was used by an 1861 South Carolina regiment in the Columbia, S.C. training area. **Dimensions:** 10½ inches tall at the tallest point. It has a diameter of 6⅝ inches at the bottom and 4⅝ inches at the top.

CONFEDERATE PISTOL: This "monster" was made from a caliber .69 Model 1842 Springfield smoothbore musket! Its overall length is 18 inches. The lockplate is marked with the eagle, U.S., and 1844. The cut-down barrel is 11⅛ inches long. Although the trigger guard and wood enclosing the barrel and lockplate have been retained, a pistol grip has replaced the original butt of the musket. This weapon was carried by a soldier from North Carolina.

CONFEDERATE SABERS AND SWORDS 49

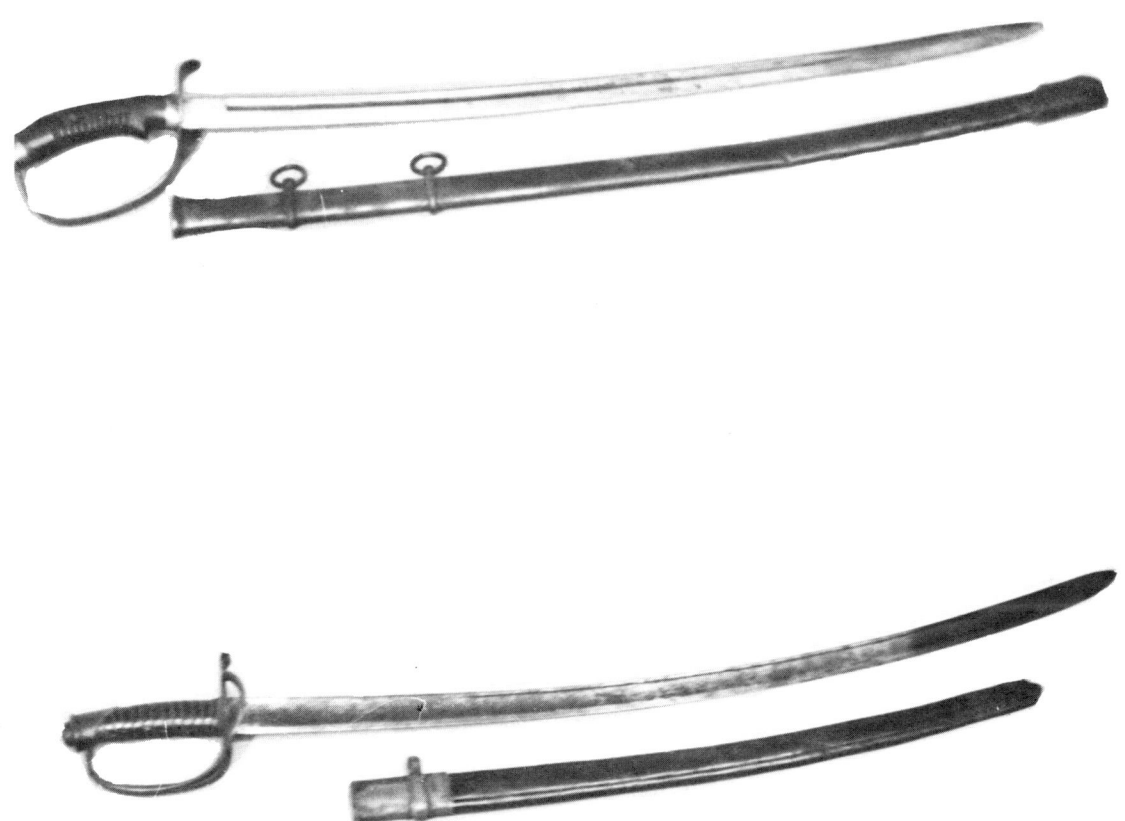

CONFEDERATE SABERS AND SWORDS: Although several excellent works on Confederate edged weapons have already been written, interesting variations still appear which merit discussion. Shown here are a C.S. saber and sword which vary in design from others previously covered in published works.

The unmarked saber from South Carolina is 40 inches in overall length, with a 31½ inch blade. It has a brass guard and an unusual grip. The scabbard is of steel.

The officer's sword was worn during the war by MAJOR HUNTER McGUIRE, 2nd Virginia Infantry, and later medical aide to "Stonewall" Jackson. This sword is 37½ inches long, with a 32 inch blade. The grip is of brass. Leather scabbard with brass furniture. No markings.

50   CONFEDERATE SHARPS BULLET MOLDS

CONFEDERATE SHARPS BULLET MOLDS: The larger mold in the photograph is a C.S. Sharps bullet mold made of crude brass. Its total length is 8½ inches. This mold is marked: **STUBS(?).** To show its size it has been photographed with a steel caliber .58 mold which is 5¾ inches long.

CONFEDERATE SOUVENIRS 51

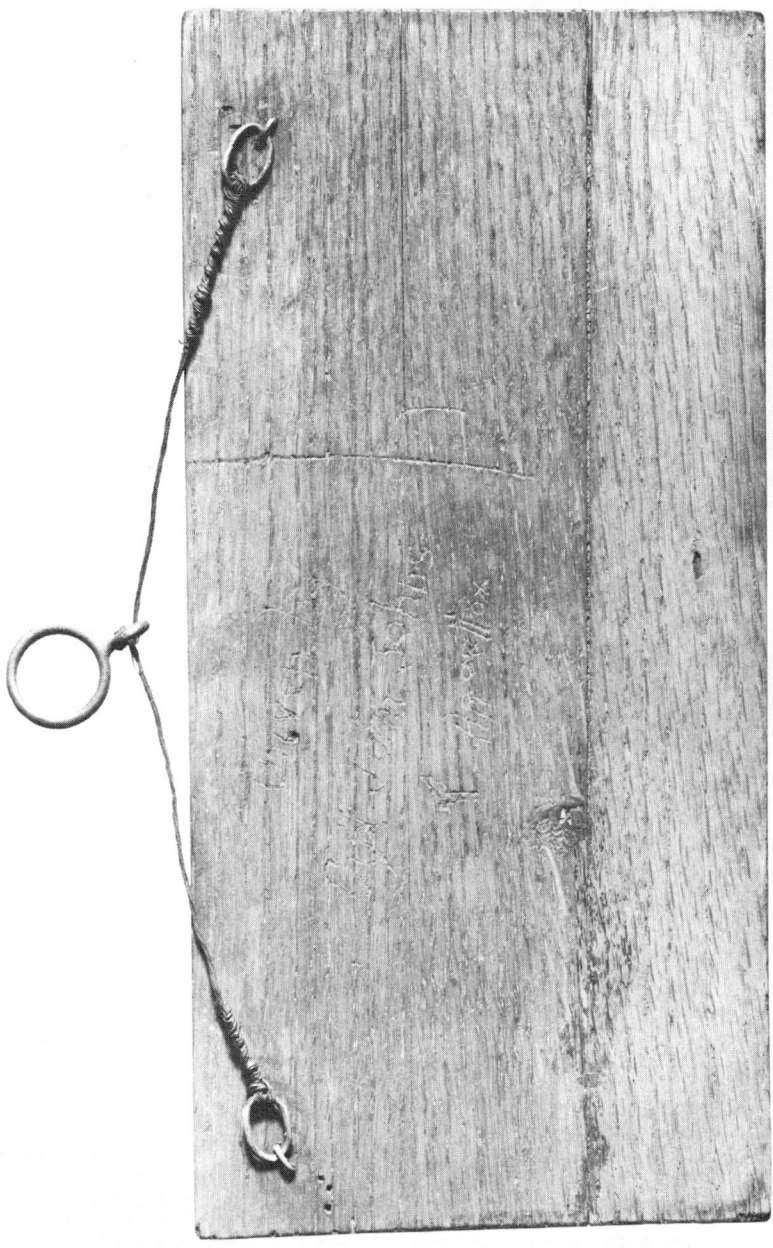

CONFEDERATE SOUVENIRS: Some Confederates were able to take home mementos of their service at the end of the war. Shown here is one such example. The Virginia belt plate and piece of battleflag were taken home after Appomattox by CAPTAIN JOHN W. JOHNS, Co. "I", "Appomattox Reserves". These relics were nailed to a piece of oak, probably part of an artillery limber seat. WILLIAM LANGLOIS; San Francisco, California]

52 CONFEDERATE SOUVENIRS

CONVALESCENT CAMP

THE CONVALESCENT CAMP at ALEXANDRIA, VIRGINIA

Although life in Alexandria, Virginia, during the 1861-1865 period has been well described in several books, the role of the city as a "staging area" for the United States has not received its just attention. This is especially true for the vast "convalescent camp" in the city which handled thousands of soldiers during the war.

Federal troops occupied Alexandria very shortly after the outbreak of war. For more than a year the city witnessed the construction of large forts as part of the series of earthworks ringing the national captial and known as the "Defences of Washington." The regiments that manned these forts as well as thousands of other troops passing through, took whatever shelter they could find or pitched their tents in the open lots and fields surrounding the city. However, as the Federal government realized the war was to be a long one, the Capital area became one huge staging area for the thousands of volunteers and draftees coming by boat and rail, especially in late summer and early fall of 1862.

Trains arrived from the north day and night and the Federal authorities had to establish a reception area for the troops as they arrived and a dispatching area for them when they left. It soon became evident that the dispatch area would also have to handle the care and forwarding of the thousands of soldiers released from the many hospitals in the area.

Two main functions were assigned to the Washington-Alexandria staging complex because of the close connections by rail with Baltimore, Philadelphia and New York. The city of Washington thus became the reception center for the new regiments on their way to the front. The role of a forwarding center was awarded to Alexandria. This was a logical choice as not only did the latter have substantially more open land to accommodate camps, it also had an excellent port for shipping troops by sea to points south. In theory the reception and forwarding of troops should have been a reasonably smooth operation. Such was not the case, however. The war grew to such a scale never imagined by the Federal military leadership thinking in terms of 1812 or 1848, and much of the responsible leadership was unimaginative and non-innovative.

Let us examine first the conditions that confronted the young volunteers as they arrived in the Nation's capital. Then we can turn our attention to Alexandria, itself. These two cities can be likened to the forward and exit ends of a tunnel leading to the war zones. A complex of buildings in Washington was the receiving end. These buildings bore such signs as "Soldiers Retreat" and "Soldiers Rest." To the thousands of travel-weary young soldiers from Maine and other points north, the sign boards must have appeared enticing — especially after their heart-warming reception in Philadelphia with its cheering throngs. But their anticipation soon turned to disgusted disappointment.

CONVALESCENT CAMP

When one reads first-hand accounts of the abominable reception given the volunteers in the Washington area, one finds it extremely difficult to explain or excuse the Nation's capital which symbolized the United States war effort. It should have been the best administered and supplied staging area of the entire war effort. Washington was, after all, the center of the war effort; here were the headquarters of Ordnance, Quartermaster and Commissary departments. The Capital was the main reception and forwarding area for the thousands of men volunteering from the northeast United States. But Washington failed miserably in aiding these men to the front. There were only poor reception facilities as the men arrived after a long, fatiguing train ride; poor housing — often not even tents — and incredibly poor food. The effect on the recruits' physical condition and morale is obvious. A sampling of soldiers' reactions to their reception is interesting, not only as illustrative of the mismanagement but also because it has not been noted in any detail before.

As early as September 1861 the 6th Connecticut Infantry arrived at "Soldiers Retreat." Here were three long rows of tables, running the length of the building, "each piled up with chunks of half-boiled pork which looked as if they had been cut from the hog when just killed for the bristles were long enough to lift up each piece by." Also present was a quantity of stale and musty bread and some very muddy coffee. The men walked out and went to eat at nearby restaurants. A month later, another Connecticut Infantry regiment (7th) found fat maggots in their beef at the "Soldiers Rest." Some men ate at these establishments more than once, having little money of their own to spend, and therefore, could compare their reactions over a period of time. When the 122nd Pennsylvania Infantry visited "Soldiers Retreat" on August 16, 1862, it found the supper to be "very scanty." But on re-visiting the Retreat on May 9, 1863, the men were provided with a "bountiful supper of fresh bread, hot coffee and the proverbial 'salt horse' — vastly different from the [first] reception."

The reaction of most soldiers was very similar to that of Robert Tilney of the 12th New York Infantry. He and his comrades were received royally in New York and Philadelphia but met a cool reception in Baltimore and "no welcome" at all in Washington. "They let us down gradually." In Philadelphia at the Cooper Shop Refreshment rooms the tables were covered with cloths, the china was clean and homelike. Everything was neat and good and was "served in a friendly manner." At Baltimore there was some effort; the food was plain but good. But, on arrival in Washington "we were sent into a shed, with a shelf along the walls and no seats. We were given bread without butter, and something which by courtesy, was called coffee. The shelves, from frequent use and infrequent cleaning, were sloppy with spilt coffee, which was served in tin cups, while the slices of bread, two or three in number, were slapped down on the wet boards." Other regiments found similar conditions.

Soldiers found conditions bad not only on their entrance to the Washington area but also during their stay and departure. In late 1862 the flow of battle casualties to the Nation's capital had created a space crisis in the hospitals in Washington. The slaughter at Second Manassas (August 29-30) and Antietam (September 17) was filling the hospitals to overflowing. A partial solution was to remove the convalescing soldiers

CONVALESCENT CAMP

from the hospitals and put them elsewhere. They could be housed with the many stragglers who left their regiments after the battles, or were separated in the heat of the battles.

Accordingly, on September 15th, the General-in-Chief H. W. Halleck, ordered Major General N. P. Banks to establish a camp near the fortifications of the capital city for housing the many stragglers in the Washington area. These men were to be organized into their companies and regiments and forwarded to their units. That same day Banks responded to Halleck's order in the following General Order No. 3 of "Defences of Washington." In brief, this order directed the military governor of Alexandria to organize immediately a "camp of convalescents, stragglers, and recruits." These men were to be organized in squads according to their original division or corps. Shelter was to be provided for the officers and men, and all enlisted men without haversacks, canteens and blankets were to be re-issued these necessities. As opportunity occurred the officers and men were to be forwarded to their regiments. About a month later (October 29) Major General George B. McClellan, in General Order No. 179, directed that "all patients discharged from hospitals at Washington, Georgetown, and Alexandria, belonging to the Army of the Potomac, [would] be sent to the convalescent camp, near Alexandria."

By mid-January 1863, the camp had 1200 men with others constantly arriving. According to a report of January 14th some 60 men were being discharged each day. It was expected that the camp would house at least 5,000 men, with a possibility of being expanded to 20,000.

As the months went by there was an ever-shifting assemblage of men waiting for transportation to their regiments and often waiting for months.

The camp facilities did not improve as time went on and soon the camp acquired the significant title of "Camp Misery." Julia S. Wheelock, a "hospital agent" made several visits to the camp. According to her, "Camp Misery" was located about 1½ miles from Alexandria proper. Her comment on the camp is indicative of the aptness of the title "Camp Misery."

> Here were 10,000-15,000 soldiers — not simply the convalescent, but the sick and dying — many of them destitute, with not even a blanket or an overcoat, having little or no wood, their rations consisting of salt pork and hardtack . . . They had no fire with which to do the cooking — consequently much of the time they were obliged to eat their pork raw."

In those days the eating of raw pork was extremely dangerous and evoked the dread of painful and fatal disease.

Another observer, Captain Robert G. Carter, in his reminiscences located the camp as occupying the original "Excelsior Hospital," located on the summit of Shuter's Hill, overlooking Alexandria, and between the Little River and Leesburg turnpikes. The captain called the camp a "burning disgrace," where a show of greenbacks procured a man's discharge from the service as easy as tumbling off a log." In the early morning the "bummers and beats" exercised up the steep hills in the vicinity, just before

CONVALESCENT CAMP

surgeon's call, and then religiously attended the call and "with hearts thumping from a hard run, and a generous display of the filthy lucre, were pronounced badly affected with heart disease and booked for what they had long desired — a journey to 'Home Sweet Home.' It was here that red ink, or some other substitute, was skillfully used to simulate blood from the mouth and lungs, or the last stages of consumption." In order to keep the men occupied they were marched out every morning to work on the fortifications. The working party usually numbered about 400 men when it left camp but about 75 when it arrived at the fort where work was to be done. The others visited the city of Alexandria or other camps. The camp was investigated by a committee of Congress but for the greater part of its existence it "remained a perfect scourge to the army."

Primarily, of course, the camp was a camp for convalescing sick and wounded soldiers. No discussion of the camp is complete without reference to the medical facilities in operation. The first hospital ward in the camp was a converted barracks. When the regiments left the Alexandria area for the front more barracks were turned into improvised hospitals. And when these buildings had reached their capacity in beds, tent wards were set up. By the end of 1864, there were 25 hospitals in the Washington-Alexandria area. The total bed capacity of this complex was 21,426.

Assisting in the recuperation of the thousands of wounded and sick patients were such semi-military organizations as the U.S. Sanitary Commission and the U.S. Christian Commission. Realizing the need for a "home away from home," these volunteer philanthropic organizations established in various key locations a type of stopping-off place where the soldier could find rest, food, and some recreation — the embryonic U.S.O. of today. These "homes" also took the soldier in off the street and protected him from the many pickpockets and swindlers who met every train of furloughed soldiers and attempted to relieve them of their money.

The Sanitary Commission organized a "Special Relief Department" which administered a whole system of "homes" and "lodges" to care for the soldiers. The Commission members visited hospitals, worked on back pay and pensions for the soldiers, and compiled a basic "Hospital Directory." Due to very faulty records the military establishment frequently had no idea where sick or wounded soldiers were being treated. The Hospital Directory, prepared by the Commission covered hospitals all over the war area. Between October 1862 and July 1864, this Directory was expanded to a total of 700,000 names!

The main purpose for the founding of the Commission had been to aid the army medical service. Some of the most prominent Commission members were medical doctors themselves. Their contribution to military medicine was very substantial. And, as close observers of the conditions at "Camp Convalescent," they inevitably became involved in the correction of the camp's evils. The Commission certainly took a forward step when it successfully secured the appointment of the very competent William A. Hammond as Surgeon General of the Army.

The Commission was especially active in enlarging the ward facilities at the camp. The east wards of Camp Convalescent were much less attractive than the wards in the

CONVALESCENT CAMP 57

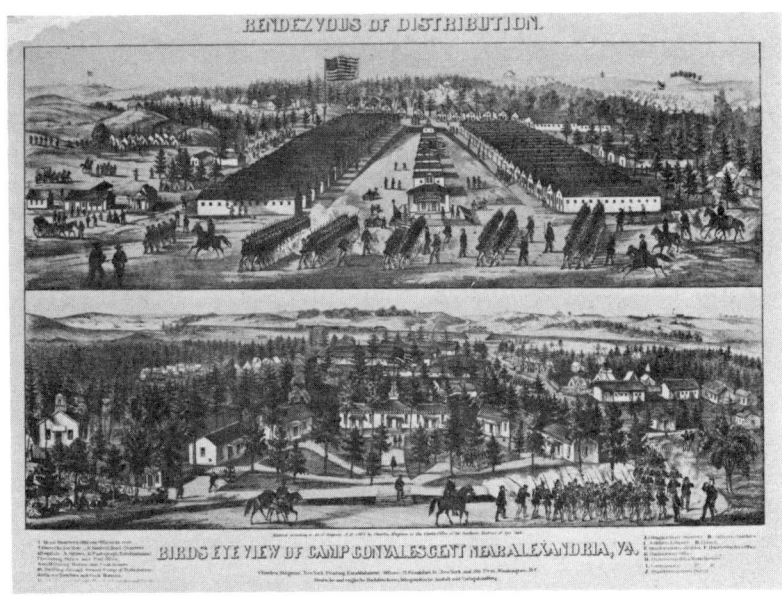

capital city, itself. The Alexandria camp had inferior housing for the men, the buildings were poorly ventilated, drainage of rain water was a constant problem. In rainy weather the camp would be a sea of mud. Death rate at Camp Convalescent was higher than at most hospitals and even some prisons.

After a few months of operation it was obvious that corrective measures were imperative. Barracks were built to get the men out of their sodden tents. Overall conditions were improved under the impetus of the Sanitary Commission with the unsung heroine, Amy Bradley, taking the lead. To support the Commission's activities, on January 3, 1863, the officers of the medical inspector's department of the Army Medical Corps were charged with the duty of making "regular and frequent" inspections of all military general hospitals and convalescent camps. (There were camps in operation in New York City and other places.) These inspections were for the purpose of determining which soldiers should receive discharges and which ones were ready to rejoin their regiments. The next month, March 24, 1863, the Army Paymaster General was directed to take "immediate measures" for the prompt payment of the sick and wounded soldiers in hospitals and convalescent camps. Some attempts were made to provide entertainment for the men awaiting official assignment for time passed slowly while the wheels of officialdom creaked forward. For example, a soldier of the 14th New Hampshire Infantry noted in his diary that Julia Ward Howe read her magnificent battle hymn, the "Battle Hymn of the Republic" to the convalescents in Alexandria late in 1864.

CONVALESCENT CAMP

In preparation of this study of "Camp Convalescent" the author was fortunate in having notes he took on conversations with this diarist who was in the camp in early 1865. He was Francis H. Buffum, and his observations were as follows:

There were some 2,000 men at the camp awaiting orders to be forwarded to their regiments. Each corps of the Army of the Potomac was represented in the camp by a street. Despite the construction of barracks, there were still a chronic shortage of housing and many men were quartered in the large Sibly tents. But after the heavy battles in the Shenandoah Valley, many wounded passed through hospitals and at the beginning of 1865, found themselves at this camp.

Buffum had been severely wounded at Cedar Creek, Virginia, October 19, 1864. After treatment in a hospital in Philadelphia (Chestnut Hill) he was sent by rail to Camp Convalescent. On his arrival, January 25, 1865, he found the food to be "quite poor" and the barracks "uncomfortable". As he noted in his diary on February 1st — although he disapproved of grumbling he could hardly believe that this camp was so poorly supplied with food and comfortable quarters as its position and importance would warrant. Finally, on February 22nd, Buffum and 700 other soldiers left Alexandria on the *Ericsson* for their regiments. The war ended a few weeks later.

"Camp Convalescent" is an example of how a good plan for care of convalescing soldiers was well-nigh ruined by red tape, bad management, and official indifference. In view of the camp's close proximity to Army headquarters and the essential service agencies, it is difficult to excuse the continuing failure in its operation. "Camp Misery" was no misnomer, many men died here. One might expect the bad conditions in a prison under enemy control, but hardly in the shadow of the capitol dome in Washington, D.C.

CROWS-FOOT 59

CROWS-FOOT: Made of cast iron and about 2 inches from point to point. This type of item was strewn in roads and in front of defense positions as a deterrent to cavalry attacks. The crows-foot would be scattered on the ground in large numbers to catch in the hooves of horses approaching the position. This was actually a very old type of primitive booby trap.

60 "CUMBERLAND" PASS BOX

"CUMBERLAND" PASS BOX: One of the very few items to survive the naval action of March 8, 1862 in which the U.S.S. CUMBERLAND (a wooden ship) was sunk by the Confederate ironclad MERRIMAC (Virginia). This pass box is of thick leather, painted orange, 15 inches tall and 7½ inches in diameter. In addition to the markings shown in the photograph the pass box has stamped on the cover — **1852.**

DAGUERROTYPE (ROUND)   61

DAGUERROTYPE (ROUND): A charming little gutta percha case, 1⅝ inches in diameter, from Ohio. The case is in two sections which screw together. The bottom section has a picture of a young lady under a glass protection while the top section has the maltese cross in the center of floral decorations. Possibly 5th Corps but more probably the maltese cross is for decoration rather than to indicate the 5th Corps. **No markings.**

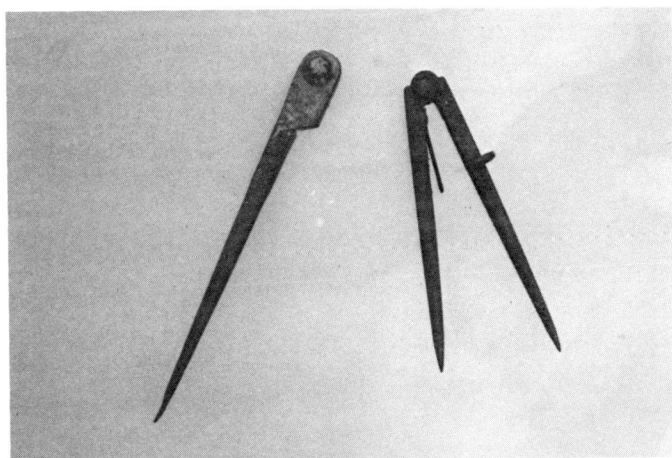

DIVIDERS: As is well known by collectors and students of the 1861-1865 war, both sides made extensive use of engineer troops. This was especially true in preparing defensive positions in the field. Many of the instruments used were very similar to those of today. The complete divider in the photograph is of iron — each "arm" is 5 inches long. Dug up at Petersburg. The incomplete specimen had "arms" 7 inches in length and was found at Spotsylvania. Recently acquired by the author is a specimen marked **U.S.** with "arms" 8 inches long. In addition to the **U.S.** this specimen is marked **8** and **P.C. TENTRAUT, NEWARK, N.J.** This divider is made of cast steel.

62 DRUM BEATERS

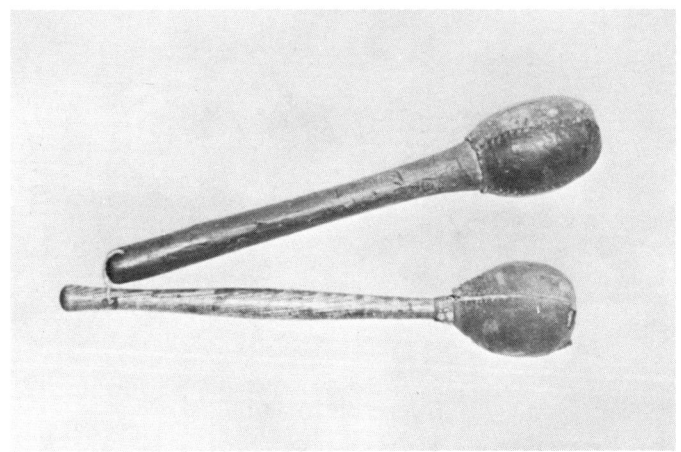

DRUM BEATERS: Rare indeed are these beaters used with the big drums of Civil War bands! These beaters are of oak with leather covering for the "beating end." Each beater is 13¾ inches long. The "beating end" is 3½ inches in length and 2¾ inches thick at its thickest point. **No markings.**

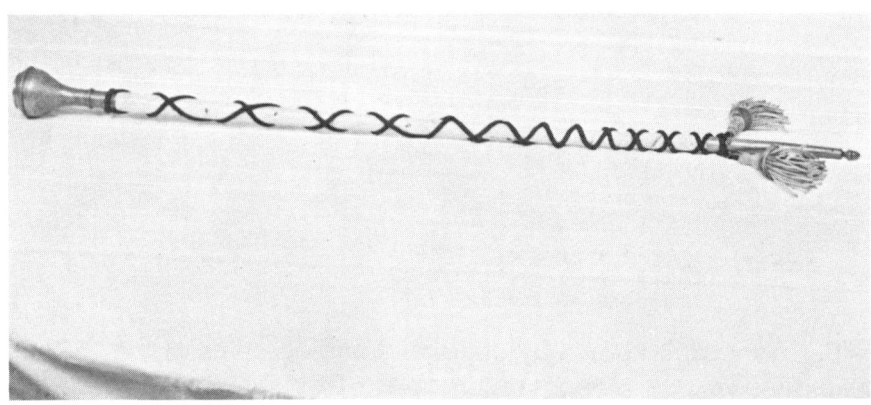

DRUM MAJOR'S BATON: A fine example of a drum major's baton carried by a Massachusetts drum major. Note the beautiful eagle which decorates the solid brass head of the baton.

DRUM MAJOR'S BATON 63

64 ENFIELD BAYONET SCABBARD

ENFIELD BAYONET SCABBARD: The mystery of Enfield rifle musket accouterments has plagued collectors for a long time. Here, at least, is a beginning in determining exactly what these accouterments were as used from 1861 to 1865 in America. This scabbard and bayonet came together in a collection. The bayonet fits the scabbard perfectly. The owner's sketch is given here without any revisions. [DAVE HOLDER; West Sussex, England]

ENFIELD BAYONET SCABBARD 65

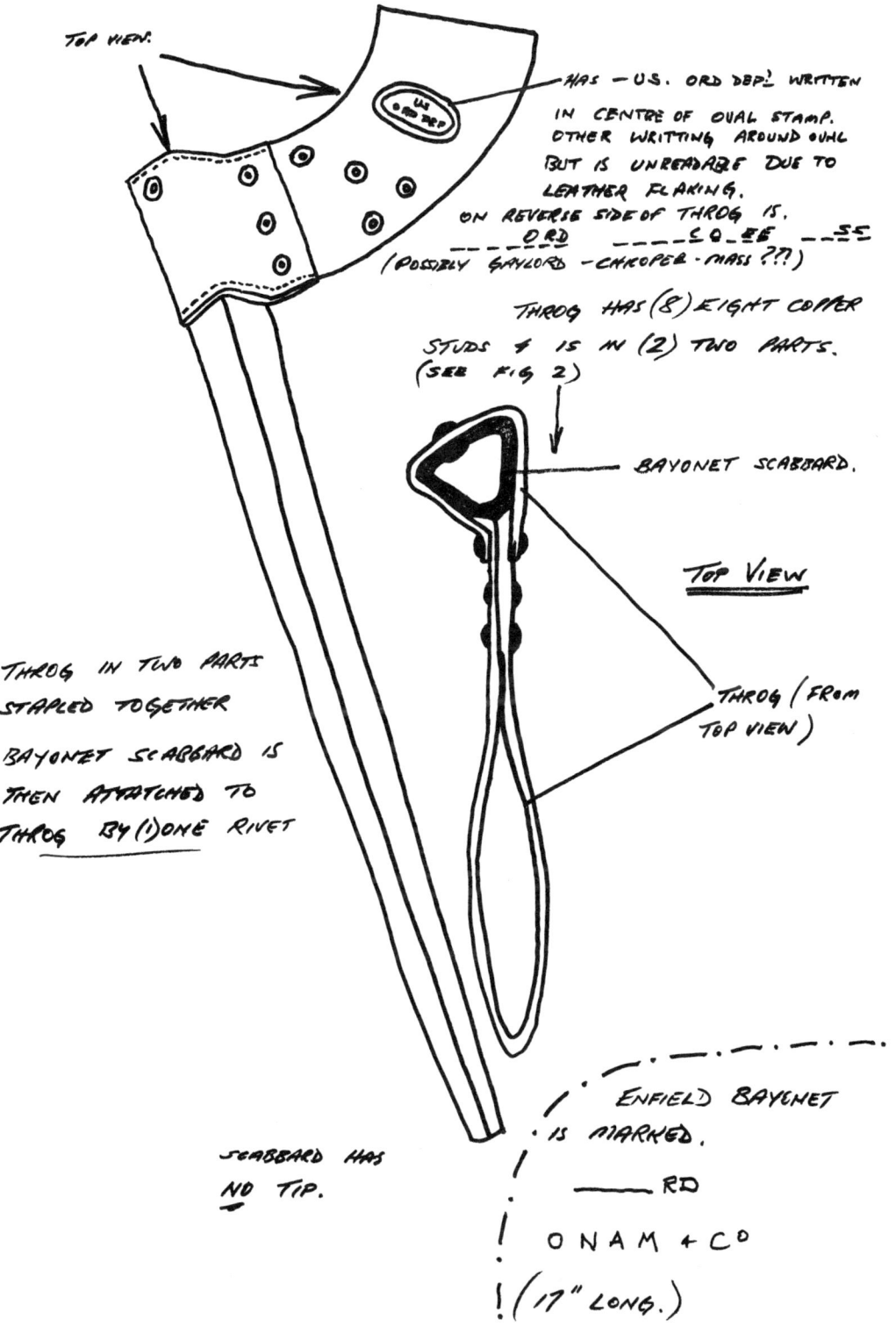

66 FAN

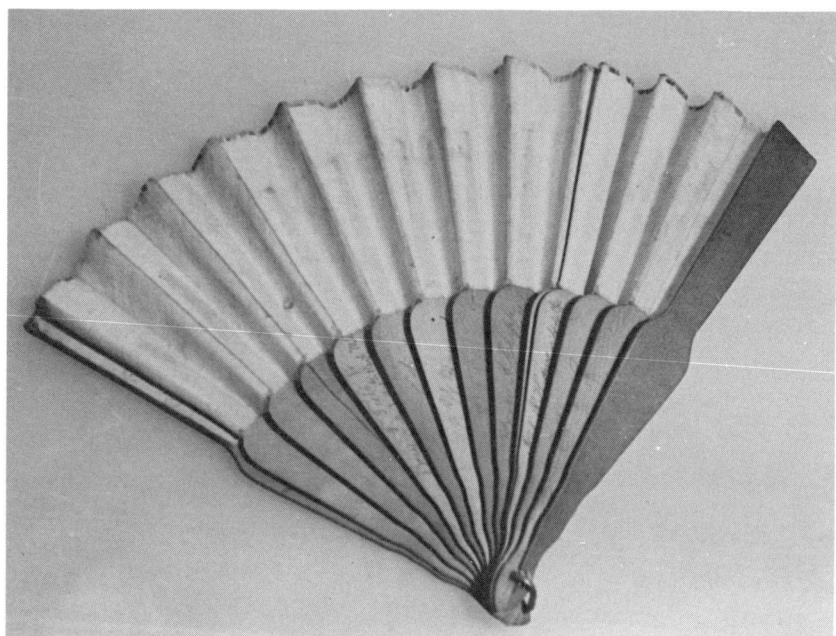

FAN: A lady's fan from a dance put on by the 44th Massachusetts Infantry. The fan is made of light wood, probably birch, with linen cloth, and has been autographed by the various regimental personnel who danced with the fair lady! This lady was Nellie Hannerde of Boston and the fan was used at a military ball at Readville, Massachusetts where the 44th was raised. The fan is about 12 inches across when fully opened.

FEDERAL SHOULDER STRAPS

There is a rich field for insignia collectors in U. S. shoulder straps. These are colorful, reasonably small and light, and often with interesting personal association. Descendants of Civil War officers often inherit the sword *and* the shoulder straps. All too frequently the uniform itself was eaten up by moths but the shoulder straps survived.

There is some confusion about what Civil War shoulder straps actually looked like. In researching for this article I have examined U. S. Army Regulations for 1857, 1861, and 1881. The 1881 Regulations are necessary to help us differentiate between the Civil War and Indian wars periods.

Collectors frequently ask me about Confederate shoulder straps. Here one must not dogmatically say that there were no shoulder straps worn by C. S. officers. It is true that the C. S. regulations, promulgated in May 1861, provided that "all indications of rank will be marked on collars and sleeves". There was no authorization of shoulder straps of any kind. But, as is well known, many Confederates had served in the "old Army". Many of these wore their old shoulder straps on their new Confederate uniforms after entering the C. S. service. Some even wore their old uniforms due to lack of the new Confederate gray. An excellent photograph of a Confederate officer wearing shoulder straps — *a year after the war had started* — can be seen on page 289, Volume 1 of *Photographic History of the Civil War*. The officer is Lieutenant J. B. WASHINGTON, a West Point graduate, who was captured May 31, 1862 while serving as an aide to Joe Johnston at Fair Oaks, Virginia.

In the Army of the United States the rank of officers was determined by the insignia on the epaulettes and shoulder straps. Epaulettes were quite gaudy and were worn mainly at dress affairs. Shoulder straps were worn in lieu of epaulettes, both in rear areas but almost universally at the front.

According to all three regulations studied (1857, 1861, 1881), shoulder straps were to be 1⅜ inches wide and 4 inches long, with an embroidery of gold ¼ inch wide. But, in practice, there was considerable diversity in size; lieutenants (perhaps characteristically!) were prone to wear unusually larger shoulder straps than called for by the regulations.

An officer's shoulder strap told three basic items of information to the observer. The *color* told the branch of service, metal insignia told the rank, and other metal insignia told the regiment or branch specialty.

According to both the 1857 and 1861 Regulations, rank was shown on the shoulder straps as follows:

                  Lieutenant General — 3 silver stars
                  Major General   — 2 silver stars
                  Brigadier General — 1 silver star

FEDERAL SHOULDER STRAPS

Captain J. Homer Edgerly

Colonel	— Silver embroidered eagle
Lieutenant Colonel	— Silver leaf
Major	— Gold leaf
Captain	— 2 silver bars
First Lieutenant	— 1 silver bar
Second Lieutenant	— Blank

These insignia were the same for all branches of the service.

The following table shows the color authorized for branches of the service as well as for the specialized branches.

Branch of Service	Color	Authorization
Infantry	Light or "Sky" Blue	1857 Regulations
Cavalry	Yellow	1857 Regulations
Artillery	Scarlet	1857 Regulations
Dragoons	Orange	1857 Regulations
Riflemen	Medium or "Emerald" Green	1857 Regulations
General Staff and Staff Corps	Dark Blue	1857 Regulations
Signal Corps	Dark Blue	General Order No. 32 Adj. Gen. Office, June 15, 1861
Chaplain	No shoulder strap authorized	General Order No. 102 Adj. Gen. Office, Nov. 25, 1861
Invalid Corps	"According to 1861 Regulations BVT worked on Dark-Blue Vel.	General Order No. 158 Adj. Gen. Office, May 29, 1863

Also, major generals were authorized dark blue for their shoulder straps, but some specimens in my collection are definitely *light* blue — and have not faded in color since the War.

FEDERAL SHOULDER STRAPS

The 1861 Regulations provided that the regimental number should be embroidered in gold on the shoulder strap. This, however, was done only in rare cases — probably for reasons of military security. Moreover, I have seen several specimens where the regimental numbers are of silver! The 1861 Regulations also provided for the following insignia for the specialized services!

Specialty	Insignia
Medical Department or "Service"	**MS** in old English characters
Pay Department	**PD** in old English characters
Engineers	Turreted castle (silver)
Topographical Engineers	A shield embroidered in gold and the letters **TE**
Ordnance	A shell and flame in silver embroidery

It was not until 1881 that Chaplains were authorized to wear shoulder straps. In that year the army chaplain was authorized to wear a shoulder strap of "black velvet with a shepherd's crook of frosted silver on the center of the strap".

Confederate sharpshooters always looked with great interest on Federals with shoulder straps! In fact, their interest frequently ended with abrupt finality, the individual's earthly career on whom they bestowed their special attention. Accordingly, many officers wore their rank designation as inconspicuously as possible. Grant often wore an enlisted man's coat while Sheridan avoided glamorous uniform accessories. A member of the 1st Maine Cavalry (Edward P. Tobie) who saw Sheridan very frequently "could not remember to have ever noticed any insignia of rank about him". Naturally, all officers dressed up when they were to be photographed. On one occasion a soldier of the 1st Connecticut Light Battery was approached for a piece of tobacco by a man in a private's uniform. The soldier gave the man some tobacco and while talking with him noted that he had the star of a brigadier general on his collar — the only mark of rank he was wearing.

Miniature insignia of rank were worn by some officers in lieu of the conspicuous shoulder straps. By General Order No. 286, November 22, 1864, the War Department permitted officers in the field to dispense with shoulder straps, but they had to continue to wear their rank designation. Some officers removed their shoulder straps altogether on going into combat.

A good example of an officer who has substituted the miniature bars for shoulder straps can be seen in the photograph of Captain E. A. Flint, 1st Massachusetts Cavalry *(Photographic History of the Civil War,* Vol. 4, page 53). The captain is wearing a 4-button enlisted man's blouse with no shoulder straps, only the miniature captain's bars. It is difficult to tell that he is an officer at all. Of course, this practice of being inconspicuous only makes sense; his men knew who he was, but why tell the enemy!

But, as if to prove that nothing had been learned from the Civil War experience, the 1881 Army Regulations provided that "officers serving in the field may dispense with prominent marks likely to attract the fire of sharpshooters, but all officers must wear

FIELD CANDLE HOLDER

the prescribed shoulder-strap to indicate their rank"! Fortunately, we did learn later as attested to by the blackened rank insignia in World War I and the "subdued" insignia in more recent times.

FIELD CANDLE HOLDER: Fits in socket of bayonet which could be stuck in the ground. The author's collection has two types — one of thin brass, the other of silvered brass. Diameter is 2⅜ inches with a beaded rim encircling the candle holder proper. The holder itself is 1¼ inches deep with a "breather" hole in the bottom. Sold by sutlers in the field. **No markings.**

FIELD DESK 71

FIELD DESK: Made of cherry wood with a brass carrying handle. The compartments are labelled for various papers — e.g. CLOTHING INVOICES, ORDNANCE FORMS, DISCHARGE PAPERS, etc.

Dimensions: 18 inches tall, 20 inches wide, and 10¼ inches deep.

Markings: On the back of the desk: CAPT. J. H. MURRAY
    Co. "M" 62 Reg Pa

Also shown here is a field desk owned by ARTHUR LEE BREWER, JR. of Durham, North Carolina. Note the different arrangement of the interior. The bottom section has been placed on top of the desk for better photographic results.

72 FIELD DESK

FIELD SIGNAL LANTERN   73

FIELD SIGNAL LANTERN: Made of japanned tin, 5 inches tall and 2¼ inches in diameter. For use in signalling the inner center is equipped with a red glass through which the candle light shows when the inner center is rotated. There are two wire loops in back for handles. These loops fold back against the lantern when not in use. No markings.

74 FIFES

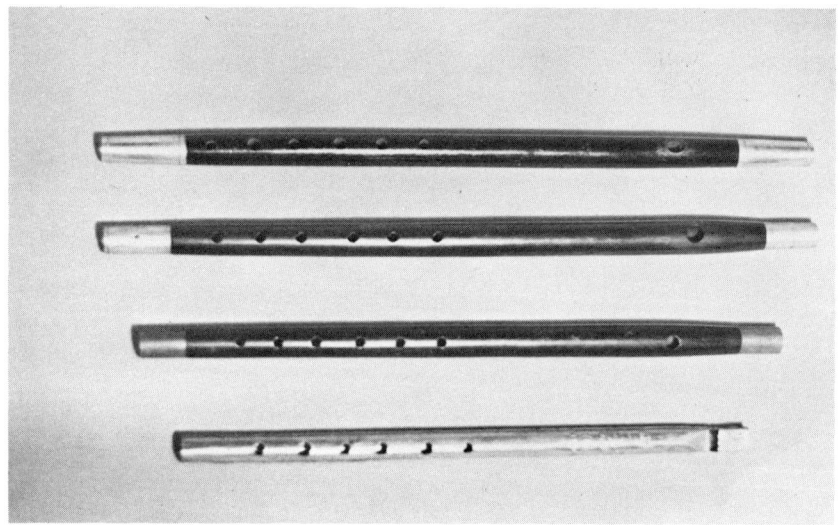

FIFES: The top fife is silver mounted, 16⅞ inches long. It is marked CROSBY.

The next fife, also silver mounted is 16⅝ inches long but with no markings. It was reportedly made under contract by William Hall & Son of 543 Broadway, N.Y. This fife was carried by Charles H. White, Co. "B" 47th Massachusetts Infantry.

The third fife from the top is brass mounted and has no markings. It came from Fort Smith, Arkansas and reportedly was used by a Confederate soldier.

The bottom specimen is a tin flute, 12⅝ inches long, decorated with **U.S.** and eagle. It is marked **ELTON** and **MADE IN U.S.A.** and reportedly was used in the Civil War.

Also shown is the rare fife mouth piece. This specimen is made of pewter. It is ⅝ inch long and ½ inch wide. There is a screw for tightening on the fife. No markings.

FISHING SINKERS 75

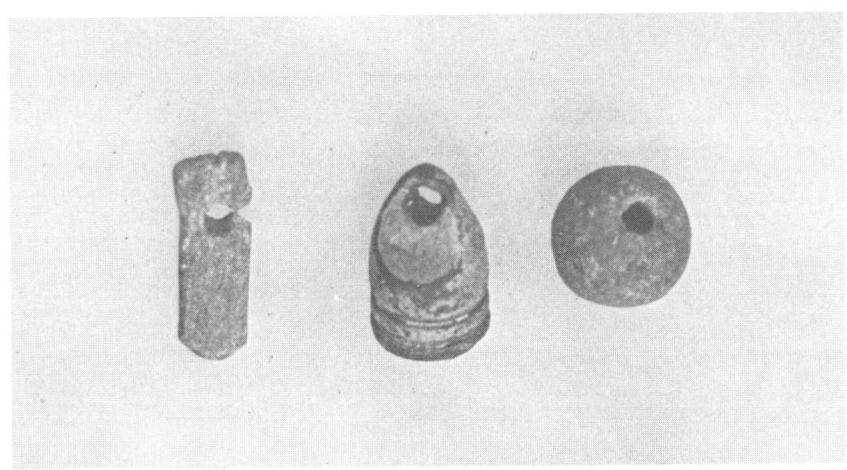

FISHING SINKERS: The Civil War was a "seasonal" war, i.e. there were long periods of inactivity between battles. Many soldiers just went fishing! Shown here are 3 "sinkers" made from bullets. The center one is from Fredericksburg and the other two are from Fort Fisher. [RODNEY O. GRAGG; Montreat, North Carolina]

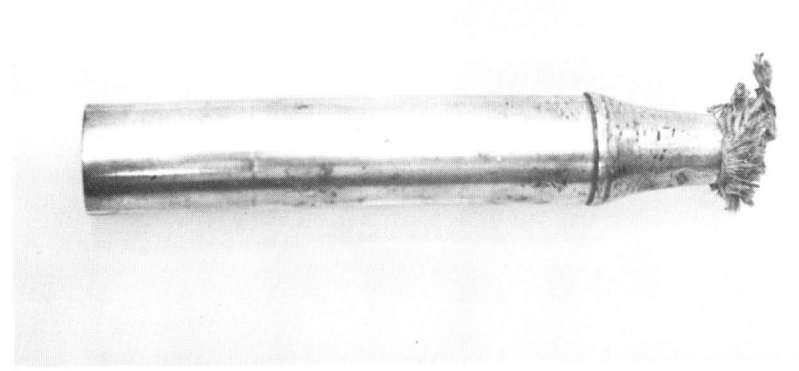

FLARE (SIGNAL?): Heavy brass flare with rope-type wick. Flare is 10¼ inches tall and 1¾ inches in diameter. A flange near the top suggests that the flare may have been inserted in a container of some sort. **No markings.**

76 FLEAM

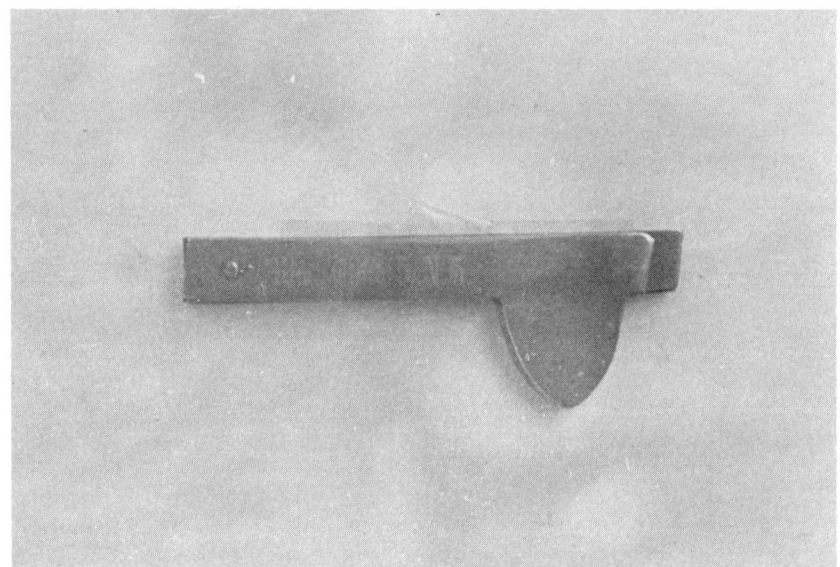

FLEAM: The fleam (or lancet) was a surgical instrument used for making small incisions. The one shown here is of heavy brass. Total length when closed is 3¼ inches. Equipped with two steel blades; each blade is 3⅛ inches long.

Markings: On one of the steel blades — R [B?] ORWICK. Also, on the brass frame — Wm. Child 5 N.H.

William Child was appointed 2nd Assistant Surgeon in the 5th New Hampshire Infantry at age 28. Promoted to Surgeon October 28, 1864. Mustered out on June 28, 1865. [DR. GERALD F. SAUER; Santa Rosa, California]

FOOTBATH 77

FOOTBATH: This certainly has to be one of the most unique items in any Civil War collection! This footbath came from Fairfield, Connecticut. It is 20 inches long at the top and 13 inches long at the bottom. The width is 16½ inches at the top and is 6½ inches deep. It is painted white inside and russet red outside. The material is a composition similar to "PAPIER-MACHE". No markings.

FROG FOR SWORD BAYONET (C.S.): A good example of C.S.-manufactured leather goods. Frog for sword bayonet, 8½ inches long. It is well made — strongly stitched. Markings: B.H. & G. CO.
ALABAMA

FUZE WRENCHES

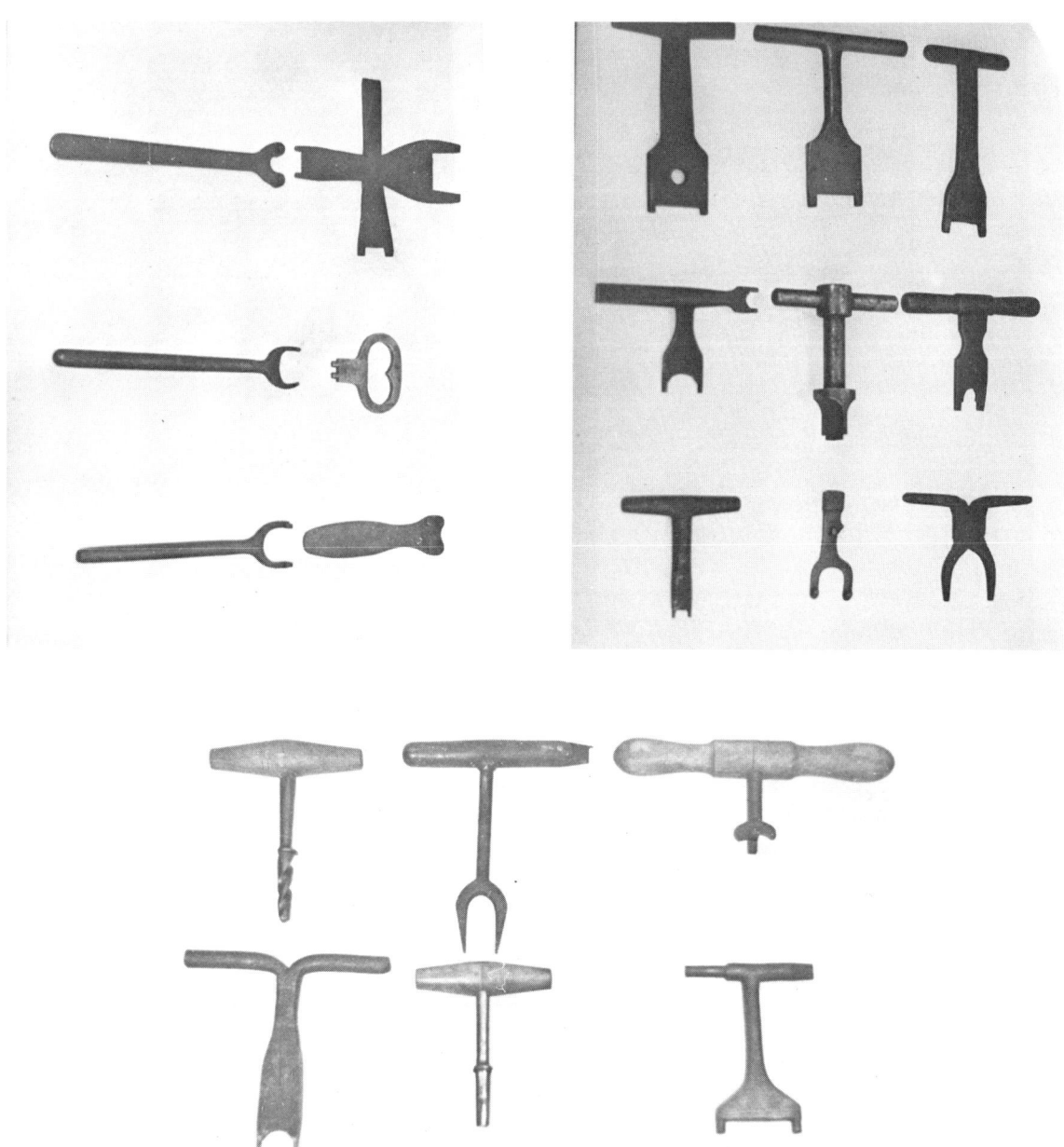

FUZE WRENCHES: The variety of these is almost endless! Shown here are some basic types but there are many more. Much work is yet to be done on these and other appendages of U.S. and C.S. artillery.

GLOVES AND GAUNTLETS 79

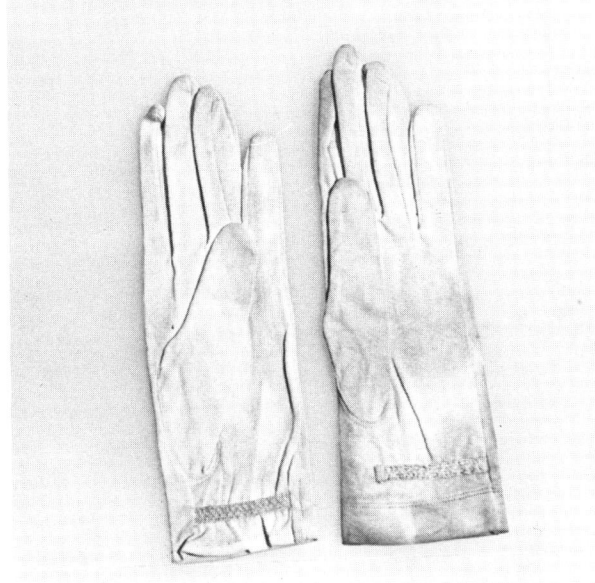

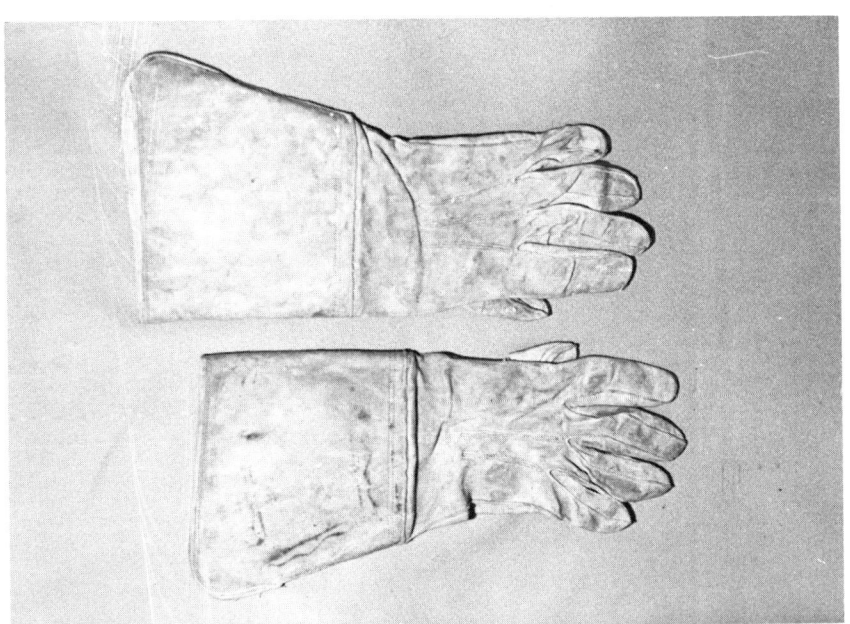

GLOVES AND GAUNTLETS: In the Army of the Potomac and on dress occasions in rear areas the Federals were required to wear white gloves. These were called "Berlin gloves" because apparently many were imported from that city. These are white cotton with a strip of elastic at the wrist. The pair shown here are 8⅝ inches long at the longest part.

Officers and some enlisted cavalrymen wore gauntlets — especially on parade. The gauntlets depicted here are buff leather, 13½ inches long at the longest point. Worn in 1861 by Captain CHARLES H. PAUL, 4th Massachusetts Infantry.

80 GRATER (POTATO)

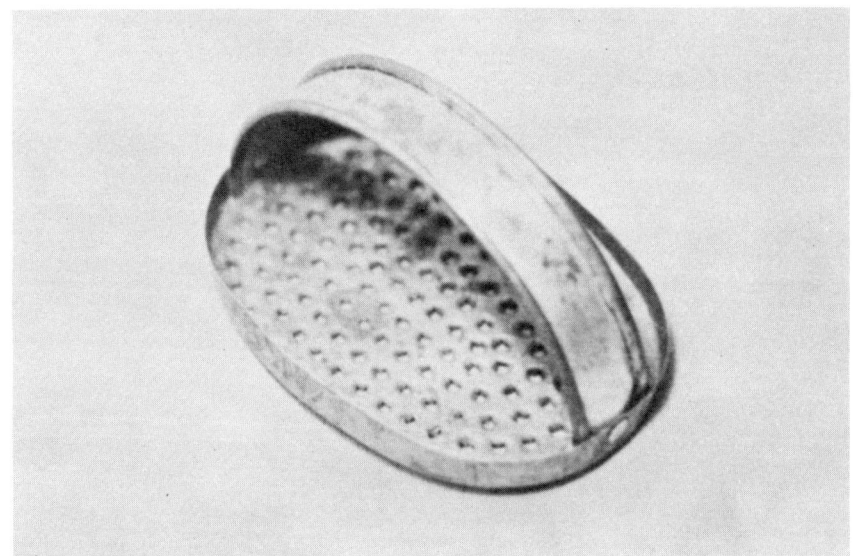

GRATER (POTATO): Tin with many perforations. 4⅛ inches long and 2⅞ inches wide at the widest part. From South Carolina. No markings.

GUN TOOLS: Often called "appendages", these are among the most baffling of Civil War items. All we can do here is show **some** of the tools known to collectors.

C.S. Spring Vise: An unusually large spring vise as can be seen with the C.S. specimen for comparison made of heavy steel — 3¾ inches tall.

Markings: 36 LA
             10   38

GUN TOOLS 81

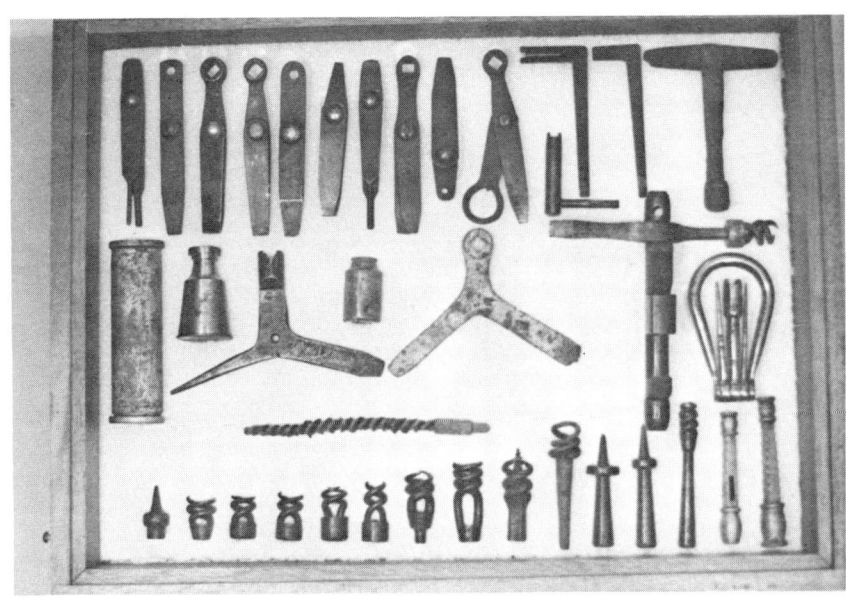

In the group picture are shown many of the more common types. They are:

Row 1 **Left to Right**
    No. 1-8 U.S.
    No. 9 Found in a Sharp's Cartridge box.
    No. 10-13 U.S.
    No. 14 C.S. from battlefield of Spotsylvania

Row 2   No. 1 Oil can and tool combination.
    No. 2 Oil can
    No. 3 Austrian gun tool
    No. 4 Oil can. The can was found on Spotsylvania battlefield; the top came from a Federal camp at LaGrange, Tennessee.
    No. 5 Gun tool from the crater at Petersburg, Virginia.
    No. 6 Musket gun tool
    No. 7 Non-regulation gun tool.

Row 3 Wire brush from Fredericksburg battlefield.

Row 4 Types of worms and bullet extractors.
    No. 9 (reading left to right) was picked up on the battlefield of Monocacy, Maryland (July 1864). Probably Confederate.

82 COMBINATION TOOL

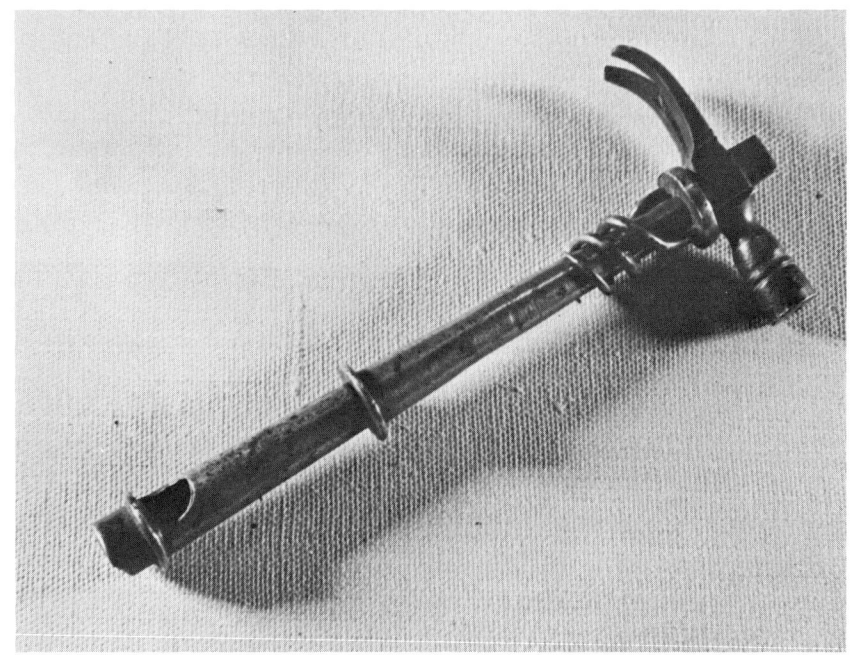

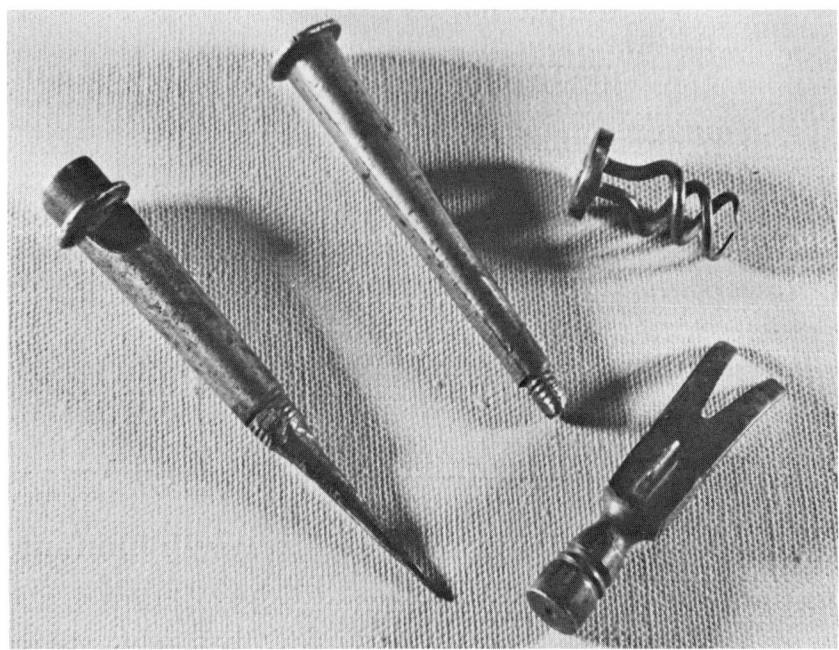

Combination Tool: Iron combination tool, probably Confederate. Each "arm" of this rare tool is approximately 2½ inches long. Rather crudely made. Photographs show tool assembled and disassembled. **No markings.** Used by Edward S. Kendall, Co. "B" 15th Massachusetts Infantry. [ROBERT CORRETTE: Fitzwilliam, New Hampshire]

HANDKERCHIEF 83

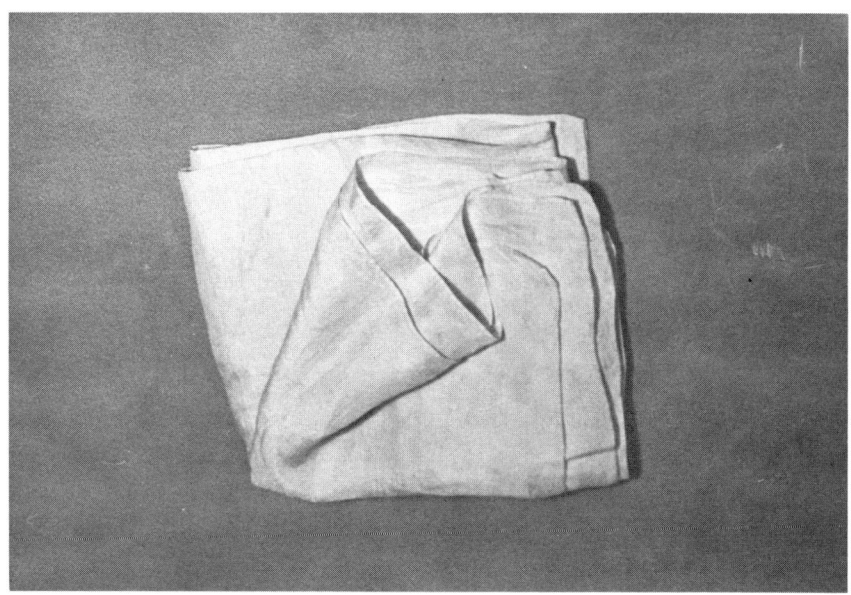

HANDKERCHIEF: Shown here is a handkerchief of the Civil War period. These handkerchiefs rank with suspenders in the high rank of **rarity.** The item shown here is of white silk, 24¾ by 27 inches. It was carried by Sergeant JOSHUA P. GRAFFAM of the 1st D.C. Cavalry.

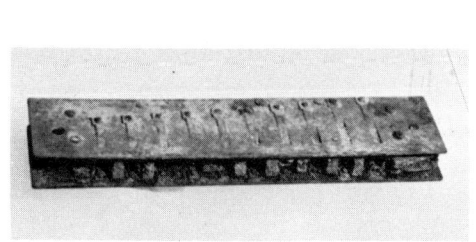  

HARMONICA: Wood is missing. Brass, 4 inches long, 1 inch wide. From camp of 7th Indiana Infantry, Fredericksburg. **No markings.**

HARMONICA BOX: Made of cardboard, 4¼ inches long and 1⅛ inches wide. Made by M. HOHNER of Philadelphia. This firm was established in 1857.

HATCHET HEADS

HATCHET HEADS: Battlefield and campsite collectors are constantly coming up with axe and hatchet heads. Naturally, the wooden handles have disappeared years ago. But here are 7 different types — and we well know there are many more!

Top Row — Left to Right
1) 5⅛ inches long with a 3¼ inch blade. Markings: **U.S.** on one side; **PLUMB** on the other. From Spotsylvania.
2) 4¾ inches long with a 2⅜ inch blade. From the Wilderness.
3) 5¾ inches long with a 3¼ inch blade. From Cold Harbor.
4) 5 inches long with a 3⅜ inch blade. From the 9th Corps area at Bethesda Church.

Bottom Row — Left to Right
1) 6½ inches long with 3½ inch blade. **Markings:** PLUMB. From the camp of 10th N.Y. Battery at Brandy Station.
2) 6⅜ inches long with a 3⅝ inch blade. The broken handle had been repaired with three nails. From Spotsylvania.
3) 6½ inches long with a 3⅞ inch blade.
   Markings: D. SIMMONS & CO
   CAST STEEL
   COHOES, N.Y.
   WARRANTED. From 5th Corps area — Wilderness.

HENRY CARTRIDGE BOX 85

HENRY CARTRIDGE BOX: Extremely rare — extremely interesting! The box is 7⅜ inches long, 4¾ inches tall and 3¾ inches tall on the inside.

Markings: U.S. on outer flap and HENRY ARMS
COMPANY
1864

86 HENRY CARTRIDGE BOX

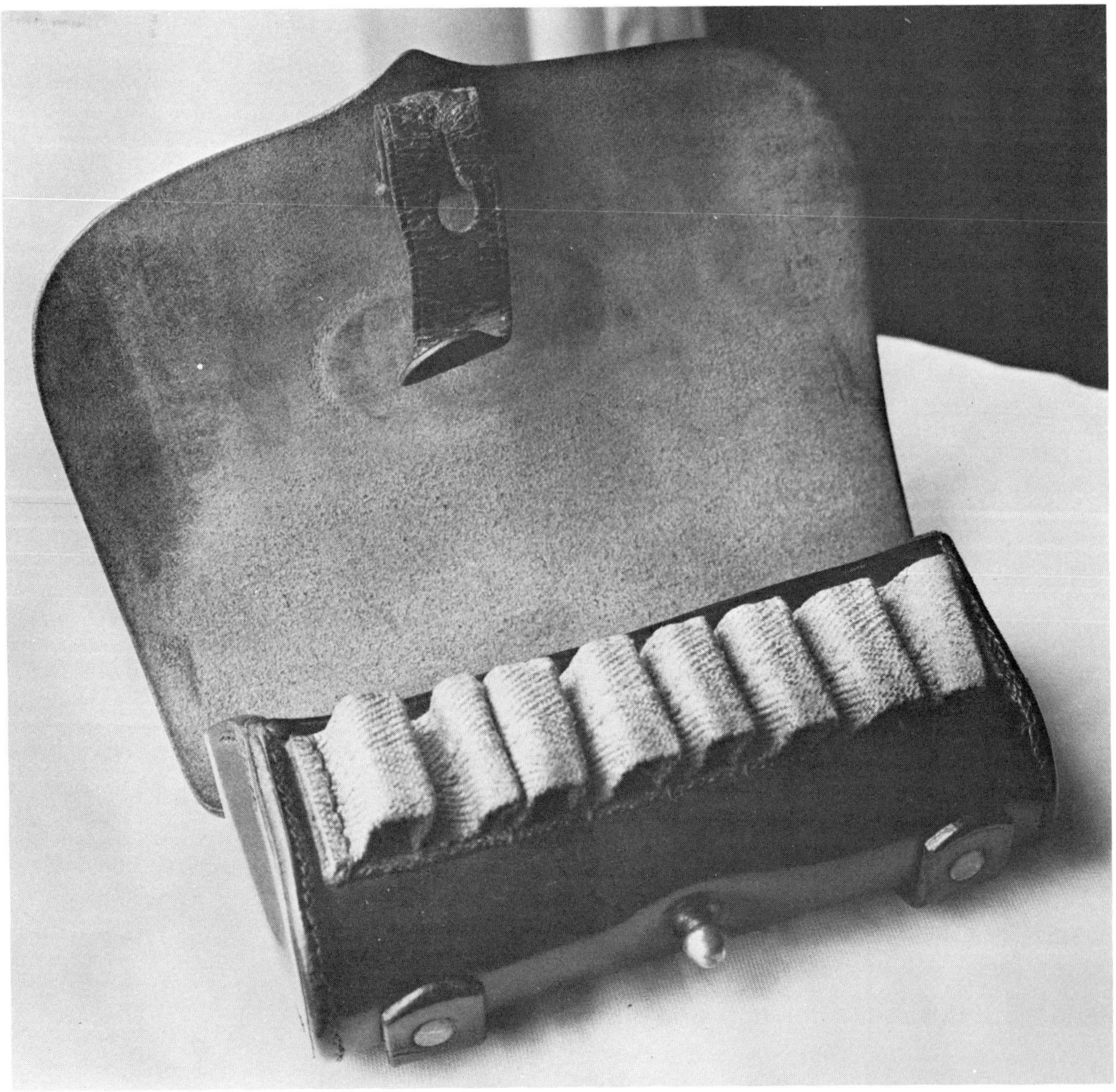

HORSESHOES 87

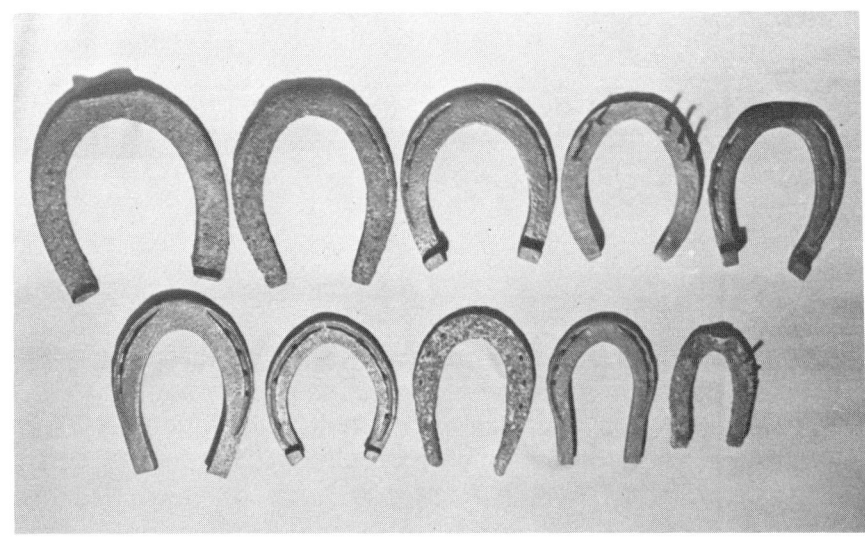

HORSESHOES: As all students and collectors well know, horses and mules were used very extensively in the campaigns by both sides. Shown here are a few of the many types and sizes of horseshoes used:

Top Row — Left to Right (All measurements are at the greatest length and width in inches.)

	Length	Width
Wilderness	7⅜	7
Alexandria, Va.	7⅛	6
LaGrange, Tenn.	6⅜	5⅝
Winchester, Va.	6	5⅛
LaGrange, Tenn. (C.S.)	6⅛	5
Bottom Row — Left to Right		
LaGrange, Tenn.	6¾	5¼
LaGrange, Tenn.	5⅝	4⅞
Corinth, Miss.	6¼	4½
LaGrange, Tenn.	5½	4
Wilderness	4½	3¼

88 HORSESHOE (MUD, SNOW)

HORSESHOE (MUD, SNOW?): An extremely odd and rare type of horseshoe from the battleground of Chattanooga. I have never seen another and do not know its original function. But it is **not** a blacksmith's creation. The shoe is 5¼ inches long, 4 inches wide, and the protuberance which extends about 3 inches below the shoe is permanently attached to the shoe in front and on both sides. **No markings.**

HOSPITAL BULLETS: The controversy still rages as to whether wounded men in the Civil War really chewed on bullets to ease their pain or not. In any event, the bullets shown in the accompanying photograph **do** have teeth marks. (Whether these are **human** teeth marks or that of animals is difficult to ascertain.) All the specimens shown are from Chattanooga except the extreme right specimen which is from Cold Harbor. [BILL HOWARD; Delmar, New York]

HOSPITAL DEPARTMENT BOTTLES 89

HOSPITAL DEPARTMENT BOTTLES: For some time now collectors have been finding U.S. Hospital Department bottles in campsites and — more rarely — on battlefields. Here are some of the more basic types encountered:

Left to Right

Amber — 9 inches tall, 3¾ inches in diameter.
Markings: U.S.A.
　　　　　　HOSP. DEPT.

Light blue — 7½ inches tall, 3 inches in diameter.
Markings: U.S.A.
　　　　　　HOSP. DEPT.

Light blue — 6¾ inches tall (excluding stopper), 2⅝ inches in diameter.
Markings: U.S.A.
　　　　　　HOSP. DEPT.

Clear — 4¾ inches tall, 1⅞ inches in diameter.
Markings: U.S.A.
　　　　　　HOSP. DEPT.

Clear — 3 inches tall (exclusive of stopper), 1 5/16 inches in diameter.
Markings: U.S.A.
　　　　　　HOSP. DEPT.

Dark blue — 2½ inches tall, 1¼ inches wide (oval).
Markings: U.S.A.
　　　　　　HOSP. DEPT.

90 HOSPITAL FLAG

HOSPITAL FLAG: Exceedingly rare U.S. hospital flag which flew over the hospital complex at City Point, Virginia 1864-1865. Brought home by the Surgeon-in-charge, ROBERT LOUGHRAN, 20th New York State Militia. (Known also as the 80th New York Infantry.) Shown also is a contemporary picture of this hospital complex; the hospital flag is shown flying under the national flag. **Dimensions:** 110 inches long and 58 inches wide. The **H** is 17½ inches long and 24½ inches wide. The color is standard as described in the first volume of the *Collector's Encyclopedia*. [SEWARD R. OSBORNE, JR.; Oliverbridge, New York]

HOSPITAL FLAG

92 IDENTIFICATION LOCKET

IDENTIFICATION LOCKET: Identification discs or — more popularly named — "dog tags" have been well described in previous publications. Here is a unique type of identification medium — a locket. It is of brass, about the size of a U.S. 25-cent piece, and has a screw-on cover.

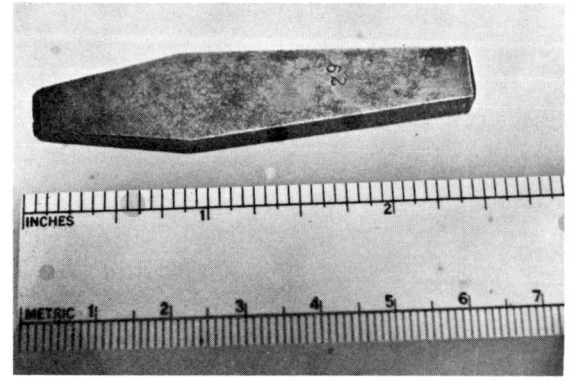 

INSPECTOR'S PUNCH: One of the real rarities! This inspector's punch is made of fine steel, 2½ inches long and ¼ inch wide at each end.

Markings: 62
                GDC

The letters refer to GILBERT D. GREASON who was an armory sub-inspector.

INSURANCE WATCH FOB 93

INSURANCE WATCH FOB: A unique dug relic. This brass watch fob was found with a U.S. belt buckle, cartridge box plate, and "eagle plate" all together in one spot in Spotsylvania. In addition to the insurance company seal, the fob has the following markings: THE OWNER OF THIS NUMBER IS
REGISTERED ON THE BOOKS OF
THE COMPANY.

INSURANCE IN ALL ITS BRANCHES
   894
1004 UNION BANK BLDG
   PGH
DUQUESNE UNDERWRITERS INC.

94 IVORY POCKET DIARY

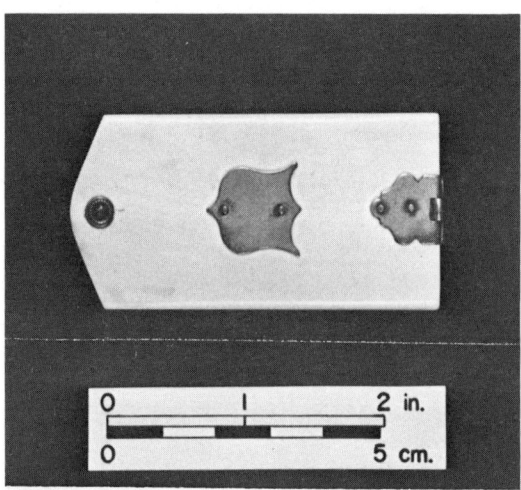

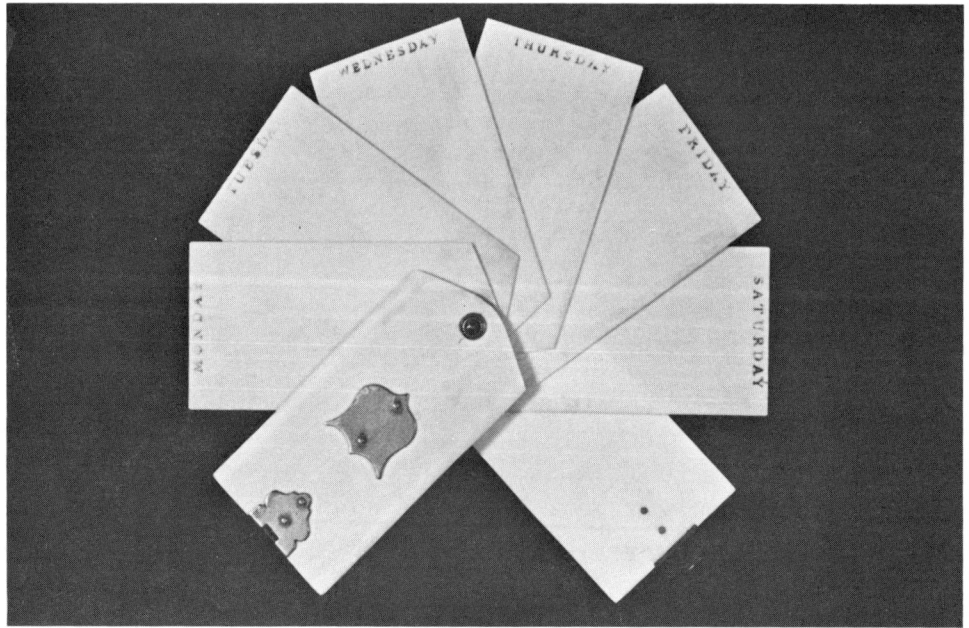

IVORY POCKET DIARY: Made entirely of ivory, cut into rectangular sheets, hinged at one end, and silver mounted with silver shield and latch. Open, the sheets fanned out allowing the owner to pencil notes on the appropriately titled page. A sheet is available and titled for every day from Monday through Saturday. When the notes were no longer needed, they were simply erased. **Dimensions:** 1 3/5 inches wide and 3 1/10 inches high. **Markings:** None. This is an exquisite little gem of a soldier's personal item and very rare.

KENTUCKY KETTLE 95

KENTUCKY KETTLE: Made of cast iron, 7¼ inches tall and 9½ inches wide at the widest point. The cover is marked: HARE, LEAF & CO.
LOUISVILLE, KY.
PATENTED
JUNE 23, 1863

96 KNAPSACKS

KNAPSACKS: Although in general the topic of knapsacks has been discussed in previous volumes of the *Encyclopedia,* these photographs of marked knapsacks merit attention. Both are regulation size and made of black waterproof canvas.

The New Hampshire item is stamped in red:

Co. B
13 N.H.

Stencilled on the inside: U.S.
1864

This knapsack belonged to HENRY C. WILLARD, Co. "B" 13th New Hampshire Infantry. Willard was promoted corporal and was wounded at Cold Harbor, June 1, 1864.

KNAPSACKS 97

The Massachusetts item is stamped:

> GLP
> Co. E
> 44th M V M

On the inside flap is stencilled:

> G. L. Pulsifer
> Co. E, 44th
> REGT. MASS.

Also: MANUFACTURED BY
JOSEPH SHORT
SALEM, MASS.
PATENT JAN. 28, 1862
SOLD BY
PALMERS & BELDERS [?]
BOSTON, MASS.

98 LEGGINGS

LEGGINGS: White canvas leggings, 13 inches tall, with an instep and 9 white china buttons on each. **Markings:** (On inside of each legging) NON PAREIL. The French lettering suggests that these may very well have come over with the shipment of Zouave uniforms early in the war.

LITHOGRAPH 99

LITHOGRAPH: A good example of the lithograph which was popular up through and for years after the war. Lithography vied with photography in getting the war scenes to the home front. The example here is entitled: SHERIDAN'S FINAL CHARGE AT WINCHESTER. It was put out by the American Lithographic Company after the war and depicts the battle scene fairly accurately. Many lithographs were highly inaccurate but they were produced by the thousands. Probably the best known producers were Currier and Ives; Prang, and Kurz and Allison. In a class of its own is the Chas. Magnus lithograph. Magnus produced many; his hospital scenes are especially good.

100 MAP READER

MAP READER: Brass map reader, 1⅜ inches tall (closed) and 2¼ inches tall (open). Diameter 1⅛ inches. Used by Sergeant Austin C. Stearns, Co. "K", 13th Massachusetts Infantry. **Markings:** PATENTED MAY 24, 1864

This map magnifer or "reader" was used by topographical engineers to magnify smaller print of creeks, elevations, terrain features, etc. There are two sections with the "eyepiece" fitting snugly over the base; the "eyepiece" can be pulled up, extended, to the desired clear magnified view of the object or printing. There are two magnifying lens in this reader.

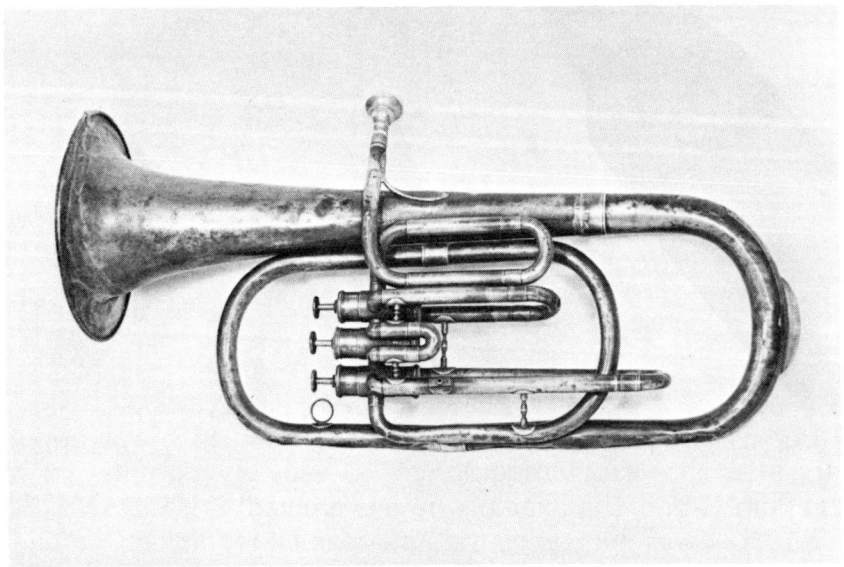

MASSACHUSETTS HORN: The brass horn shown here was carried by Warren Gilchrest, a member of the band of the 1st Massachusetts Infantry. **Dimensions:** 25¼ inches long and 8¼ inches in diameter at the "bell" of the horn.

MEDICAL FLASK 101

Markings:

JOHN F. STRATTON
NEW YORK

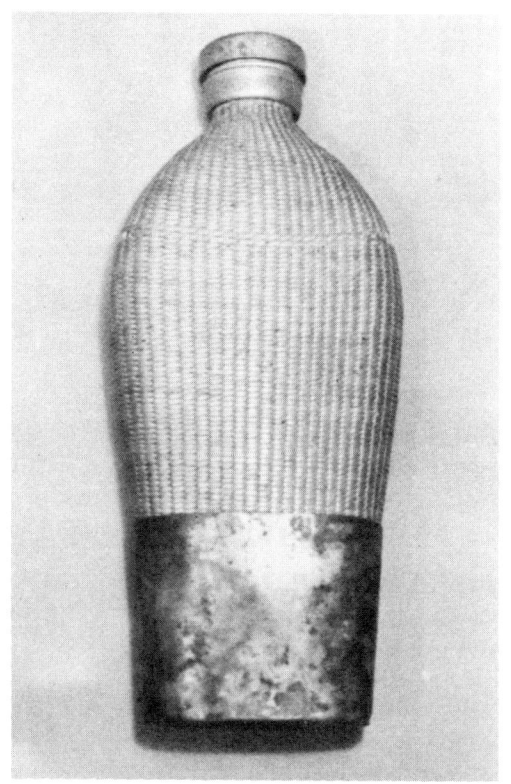

MEDICAL FLASK: Unusually large flask used by medical officers for brandy for patients undergoing surgery. Made of pewter and covered with wicker. The flask is 9½ inches tall and is equipped with a pewter cup 2½ inches tall. This flask is much larger than the pocket flasks carried during the war. From Antietam. **No markings.**

102   MESS KITS

MESS KITS: The amazing variety of Civil War mess kits continues to intrigue the collector. Eventually, some dedicated, research-inclined individual will come out with a definitive treatment. Here are a few "new discoveries" since the publishing of early volumes of the *Encyclopedia*.

Mess Kit — Canteen Combinations: Consists of four tin utensils which can be assembled for carrying. The carrying apparatus is of thick black leather with a shoulder sling 4½ feet long. The utensils are:

- **Canteen** — Height 7¼ inches; width 5 inches at bottom, tapering up to 6 inches at widest point; 2½ inches deep.
- **Pan** — No handle. Length 7¾ inches; width 5¾ inches at bottom, tapering up to 6¼ inches at widest point; 3 inches deep.
- **Pan** — Similar to above pan but equipped with a folding handle 5½ inches long.
- **Soup Pan** — Equipped with two folding handles. This pan is 6⅛ inches long; 2½ inches wide, and 4 inches deep.

No markings.

MULLIGAN'S PATENT MESS KIT

Mulligan's Patent Mess Kit: Made of tin. Height 5¼ inches. Bottom part is a mess pan 4⅝ inches in diameter and 2½ inches deep. Its cover forms a smaller pan 1⅝ inches deep over which fits a tin cup 3⅝ inches in diameter and 2½ inches deep. This cup is similar in shape and design to the "normal" Civil War tin cups. There are two metal loops on the bottom mess pan, apparently designed both as handles and to hold a strap. These loops are one inch wide. No markings.

104 MESS KIT OF A CONN. OFFICER

Mess Kit of a Conn. Officer: The leather container is stencilled:
   LT. WILLIAM E. PHILLIPS
   Co. "K" 7th Conn. Inf.

Phillips was captured in July, 1863 at Battery Wagner. The leather top is stamped:
   TOBIAS & WALL MAKERS
      BOSTON

The metal lid of the pot is stamped: PAT 1861. The three half-moon containers have scratched in their tops **COFFEE, CREAM, SUGAR.** Each container shows a little evidence of the content. [T. SHERMAN HARDING, II; Orlando, Florida]

Confederate Mess Kit: Another interesting mess kit is described by VERNON SCOONE of Baltimore, Maryland. (Unfortunately, no photograph of this mess kit is available for inclusion in this book.) On one side the mess kit is marked: 27 NCT. This refers to the 27th Regiment, North Carolina Troops. The size is 9½ inches long and 4 inches high. It is oval shaped, all tin, with a leather sling and roller buckle.

MILITIA BELT 105

MILITIA BELT: Patent leather belt 32 inches long, 1¾ inches wide, Brass, 2-piece buckle, stamped WOBURN MECHANIC PHALANX. Worn at 1st Bull Run by Captain J. H. PARKER, 5th Massachusetts Volunteer Militia.

MILITIA BUCKLES:

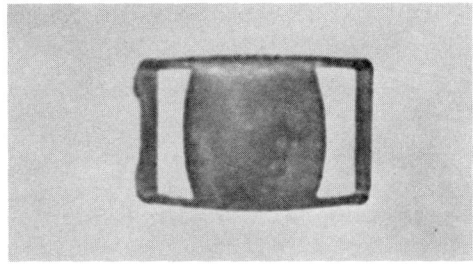

Louisiana Buckle: Made of thin brass. It is 3 inches long, 2 inches wide, and was recovered from a Louisiana regiment's position at the battle of Shiloh.

106 MILITIA BUCKLES

U.S. militia or non-regulation. Gold-plated, 2 inches tall and 1⅞ inches wide. A real beauty! [J. W. LEECH; Grand Junction, Colorado]

SOUTH CAROLINA BUCKLE 107

South Carolina Buckle: Made of heavy brass, 2 15/16 inches long and 2⅜ inches wide. Each of the letters **S** and **C** is ¾ of an inch high. The letters are brass but the palmetto tree decoration is silver. **Markings:** Scratched on the back of the buckle is the name: D. J. COLE. D. J. Cole first served in Captain Millet's company, 20th S.C. Militia. On August 1, 1863 he enlisted in the 4th S.C. State Troops. Reportedly he was captured and exchanged the buckle shown here with the U.S. buckle worn by his captain. [WILLIAM LANGLOIS; San Francisco, California]

108 SOUTH CAROLINA BUCKLE

C.S. MILITIA BUCKLE 109

C.S. Militia Buckle: Shown here are front and rear views of a Virginia (?) militia company's buckle. The buckle was made by ROBINSON ADAMS COMPANY, Richmond, Virginia. [R. V. CROFOOT; Orlando, Florida]

110 C.S. MILITIA BUCKLE

MILITIA CARTRIDGE BOXES 111

MILITIA CARTRIDGE BOXES: Here again — in this field of Civil War militia cartridge boxes — there is much to be done! Shown here are 12 such boxes. Most are of patent leather; the largest is 7¼ by 5 inches; the smallest is 6½ by 3½ inches. Most have wooden blocks holding from 16 to 18 rounds of ammunition. Three of these boxes were made by BAKER & McKENNY, NEW YORK. The others are unmarked.

112 ACCOUTERMENT DELUXE

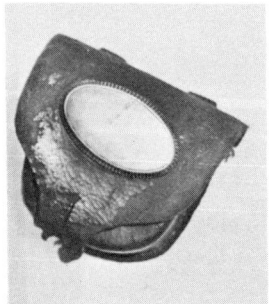

Accouterment deluxe: A regulation cap box and cartridge box but with silver plates. The cartridge box and cap box plates are the same size — 2¼ by 1⅜ inches.

Markings: Cartridge Box — WATERTOWN
ARSENAL
1864

Cap Box — C. S. STORMS
MAKER N.Y.

PENNSYLVANIA CARTRIDGE BELT   113

Pennsylvania Cartridge Box: Carried by a soldier named GREIER who served in a Pennsylvania regiment at Gettysburg. (Quite possibly his unit was part of the "emergency troops".) The cartridge box contained a pen and a New Testament. **Dimensions:** 9¼ inches wide, 5½ inches high, 3¼ inches deep. **Markings:** On the flap under the cover — 1861.

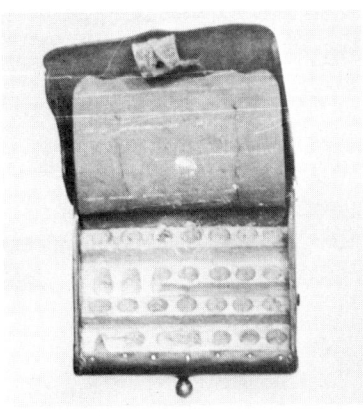 

Confederate Militia (?): A black leather cartridge box, 6¼ inches wide, 5½ inches high; 2¼ inches deep. Contains a wooden block for 28 paper cartridges. Scratched on the outer flap: 1794
                N.W. KUSS (?)

114 MILITIA INSIGNIA

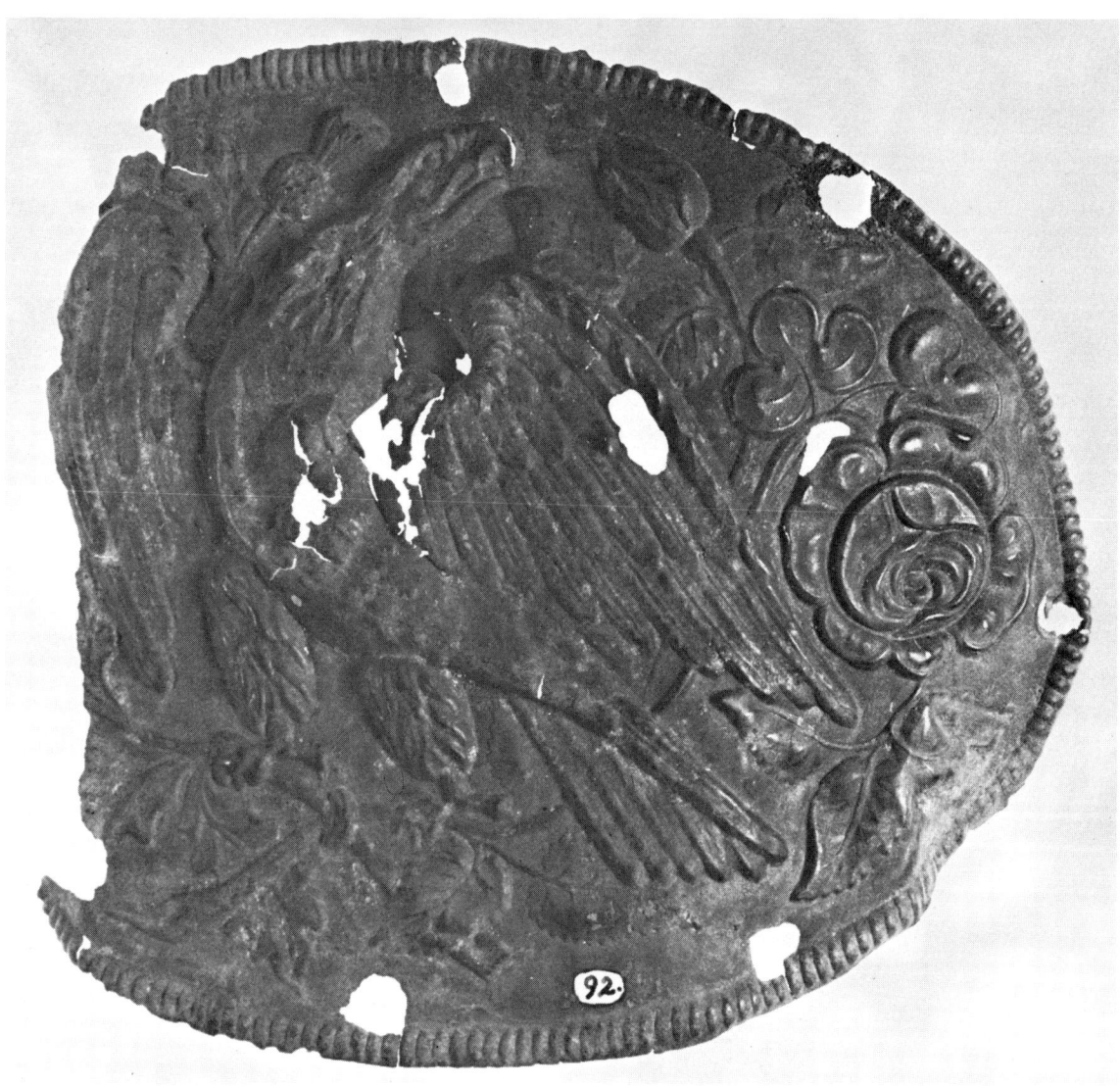

MILITIA INSIGNIA: Shown here are three examples of militia insignia.

Brass Eagle Plate: Brass eagle plate found at Fort Fisher, N.C. It is 5½ inches high and if complete, 8 inches long. Use of this plate is unknown. [TOM S. DICKEY; Atlanta, Georgia]

HAT INSIGNIA 115

Hat Insignia: Gold-gilted eagle used as a hat ornament, 1¼ by 1¼ inches in size. Found in a New York regimental camp site. [DAVID M. MORROW; Woodbridge, Virginia]

South Carolina Palmetto Insignia: From the coattails of a militia uniform coat of South Carolina — possibly as early as 1835. Some of these militia uniforms were still being worn when hostilities broke out in April, 1861.

116 TRENTON RIFLE MUSKET BOX

MUSKET BOX: Very few musket boxes survived the war. They were made of pine wood and made excellent kindling for camp fires! However, here are two "survivors".

Springfield Rifle Musket Box: Made of pine boards, 1-inch thick, painted grey. **Dimensions:** 5 feet 2 inches long. 17¾ inches wide and 13½ inches deep (without the lid). **Markings:**   20
            No BAYONETS
            SPRINGFIELD
            RIFLE MUSKETS
                CAL. 58
            1st CLASS

RIFLE MUSKET BOX 117

Trenton Rifle Musket Box: Made of pine boards 1-inch thick, unpainted. **Dimensions:** 5 feet, 1 inch long, 17¾ inches wide, and 13½ inches deep (without the lid). **Markings:**
```
         20
   RIFLE MUSKETS
      CAL. 58
   TRENTON F. A. CO.
    STAMPED N.J.
```

118 NAVAL CANNON LOCK

NAVAL CANNON LOCK: Federal naval cannon lock (hammer) recovered from the site of a U.S. Navy battery on Maryland Heights. [TOM S. DICKEY; Atlanta, Georgia]

NAVAL CAP 119

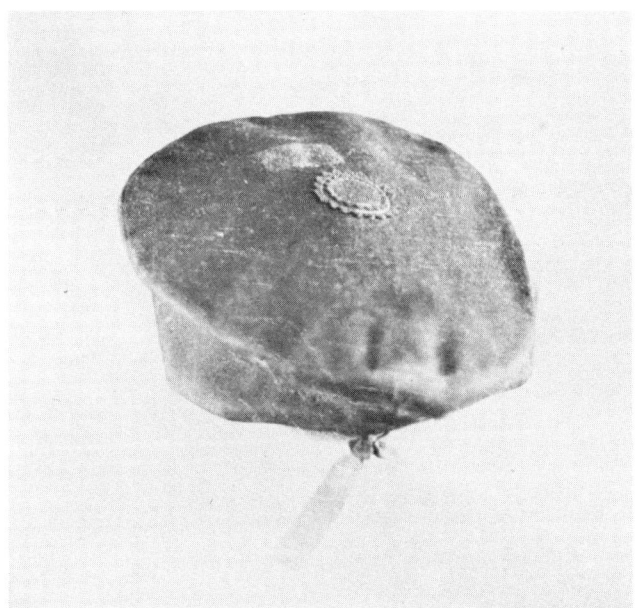

NAVAL CAP: Items of naval uniforms are rare, even for the Federal navy. Shown here is a seaman's cap of the U.S. Navy during the Civil War. Heavy blue cloth, 9¼ inches in diameter at the crown or top, and about 3½ inches deep. There is a black silk ribbon tied in a bow at the back of the cap. This ribbon is about ¾ of an inch wide. No decoration except a circular cloth design (1½ inches in diameter) is sewed in the middle of the top of the cap. **No markings.**

120 NAVAL MESS KNIFE

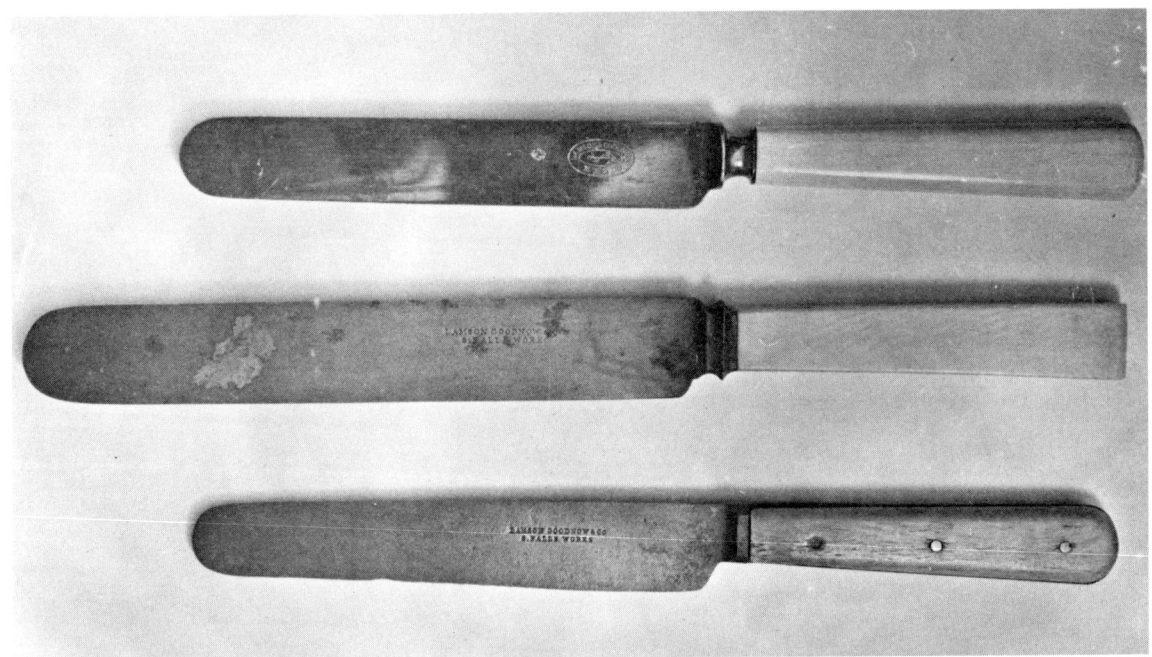

NAVAL MESS KNIFE: This knife is shown here (at top) along with two Army mess knives. All three were made by LAMSON AND GOODNOW of Shelburne Falls, Massachusetts. This famous cutlery firm was established in 1842 and by 1860 was the largest cutlery manufacturer in the United States.

The Navy specimen is 8½ inches long and has an ivory handle. It is marked in an oval with **LAMSON & GOODNOW MFG CO** and an anchor. Shown here through the courtesy of R. V. Crofoot of Orlando, Florida.

The center specimen is 9¾ inches long and also has an ivory handle. Marked LAMSON GOODNOW & CO.
    S. FALLS WORKS

The bottom specimen is 8¼ inches long with a **wood** handle. It is marked:
LAMSON GOODNOW & CO.
S. FALLS WORKS.

This knife was carried in the war by GEORGE WHITMAN, Co. "A" 27th Michigan Infantry.

NAVAL SHRAPNEL FUZE BOX   121

NAVAL SHRAPNEL FUZE BOX: As with so many wood containers of the Civil War period, this fuze box is excessively rare! Made of heavy pine boards and measures 10 by 10 by 10 inches. Rope handles. **Markings:** 8 INCH
SHRAPNEL
5 SEC
ORD. 1864

The markings also include the navy anchor.

122 NAVAL SIGNAL LIGHT (?)

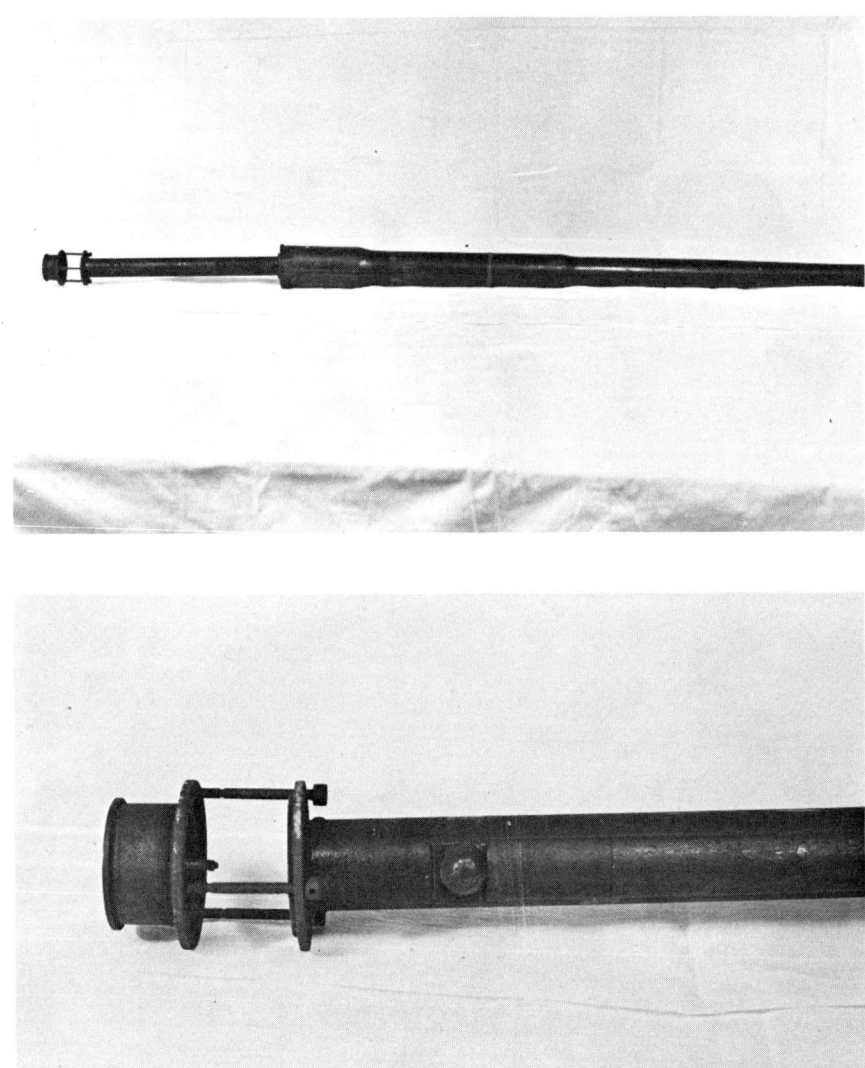

NAVAL SIGNAL LIGHT (?): This unusual light is presumed to be for naval use. It is 4 feet 7 inches tall. The bottom section is of light wood which in turn separates into 3 sections which are hinged so as to form a tripod. The "light" proper is only about 3 inches tall with the open section 1½ inches tall. The glass has been broken out. **No markings.**

NEEDLEWORK 123

NEEDLEWORK: A very charming example of Civil War period needlework. It was done in South Carolina and very probably by a young (and patriotic!) lady. The colors are still fairly bright. **Dimensions:** 19¾ inches long and 18⅛ inches wide. **Markings:** 1861
M.K.T.

124 NEW HAMPSHIRE DRUM

NEW HAMPSHIRE DRUM: This is a non-regulation drum used by a member of the 12th New Hampshire Infantry band. **Dimensions:** 14 inches tall and 24½ inches in diameter. **Markings:** Painted on the side of the drum is a shield and 12 N.H. Inf.

NEW YORK SOLDIER'S BLANKET   125

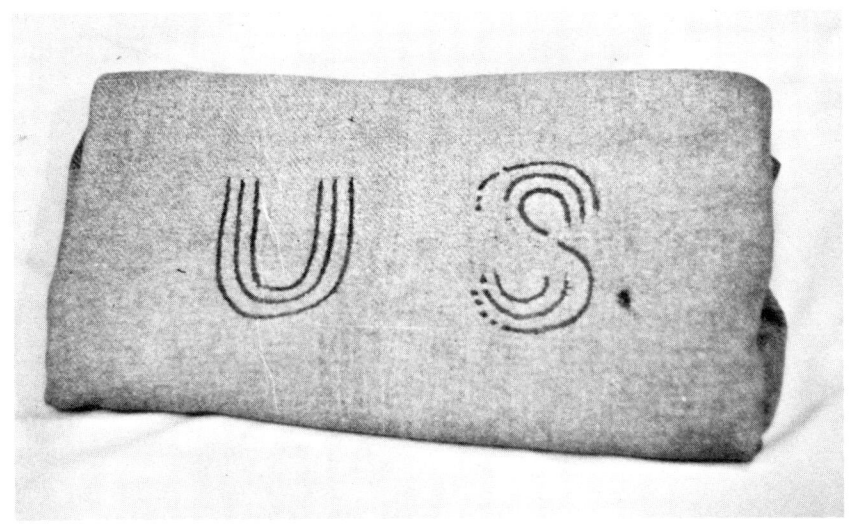

NEW YORK SOLDIER'S BLANKET: Made of **very** coarse light brown material, much resembling the material used in a horse blanket! This blanket is 6 feet 9 inches long and 6 feet wide. The letters **U.S.** in the center of the blanket are 5½ inches tall and 4¼ inches wide. Carried during the war by THEODORE J. SOUTHWORTH, Co. "A" 184th New York Infantry.

126 NOSEBAG

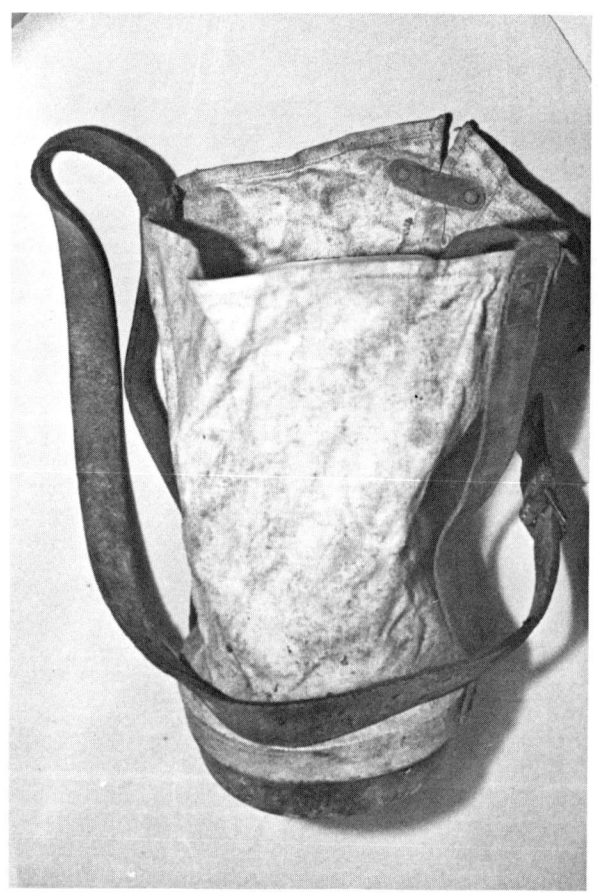

NOSEBAG: These were extensively used in both armies since it was definitely a "horse war". The specimen shown here is of white canvas with a leather bottom; and is 13½ inches tall. Equipped with a black leather strap.

Markings: on bottom — MANUFACTURED
                          BY
                 J. E. CONDICT
                 57 WHITE ST.
                 NEW YORK

NUTCRACKER 127

NUTCRACKER: Used obviously only in rear echelon establishments and on the home front. Made of cast iron, with a length at the base of 8½ inches. **Markings:**
BATTLE OF CHATTANOOGA
        1863
[TOM RYAN; Nashville, Tennessee]

128 OFFICER'S HOUSEWIFE

OFFICER'S HOUSEWIFE: Most of the "housewives" of the Civil War era were made for the enlisted man. Here is definitely a deluxe specimen which was of much better material and contents than the ones made by mothers, sisters or sweethearts. This specimen is leather covered, 3¼ inches tall, 3 inches wide and 1¾ inches deep. It is very finely made! There is a mirror in the cover and it contains scissors, a thimble, tweezers, a nail file, a small glass vial, a metal toothpick, and a holder for pen points. Truly a classy outfit! **No markings.**

OIL CAN 129

OIL CAN: Made of heavy tin with handle. It is 4¾ inches tall, 3¼ inches wide and 1¾ inches deep. The pouring spout screws into the can and the spout itself has a screw on top secured by a chain. No markings.

PADLOCKS

PADLOCKS: Every lock shown here was used in the Civil War. Several specimens are stamped **U.S.** to show government issue if not manufacture. The locks were used primarily for protecting magazine storage areas, buildings, paymaster's safes and satchels privately owned. All the measurements are at the longest and widest points.

Top Row — Left to Right:
1) 4¾ by 3¼ (steel). **Markings:** VR CROWN   COLUMBIA, S.C.
   A. THOMPSON   [ARSENAL]

2) 4¼ by 3 (steel). **Markings:** U.S.
   ST. LOUIS, MO.

3) 3½ by 2 1/3 (steel). **Markings:** V.[?3W CO.]
   Spotsylvania

4) 3¼ by 2½ (steel). **Markings:** THOMPSON & CO.
   Fredericksburg   NEWARK

Second Row:
1) 3¼ by 2½ (steel). **Markings:** W. W. & CO
   Fort Morgan, Ala.

2) 3½ by 2½ (steel). **Markings:** D. M. & CO
   Fort Morgan

3) 3½ by 2⅝ (steel). **Markings:** PATENT V.R. CROWN
   Fort Morgan

4) 3½ by 2½ (steel).
   Chancellorsville

Third Row:
1) 4 by 2⅝ (brass)
   Libby Prison — Luray, Virginia Museum

2) 3¼ by 2⅜ (brass)
   Washington Naval Yard, 1861-1865

3) 2⅛ by 1⅜ (brass). **Markings:** RITCHIE & SON
   Maj. S. K. Williams   NEWAR, N.J.
   Ohio Cav

4) 1⅝ by 1¼ (steel)
   Champion's Hill

Bottom Row:
1⅛ by ¾ of an inch (brass). No markings.
Maj. S. K. Williams
Ohio Cav

PADLOCKS 131

132 PAINTING

PAINTING: Samuel Bell Palmer on March 1, 1862, joined "Mabry Artillery" of Tennessee. Was captured and sent to Federal prison camp at Camp Douglas, Illinois. While there, a Federal officer, Major Samuel K. Williams, Jr. befriended Palmer and provided him with materials to paint. This painting is one of the results — it was painted in the prison camp and presented to Major Williams who also provided Palmer with tobacco and "other luxuries". The two men remained friends after the war.

Major Williams had been in service since 1861. In late 1864 he was ordered to Camp Douglas. Discharged September 9, 1865.

PALL BEARER'S BADGE 133

PALL BEARER'S BADGE: Black silk 10 inches long including gold tassels. Worn at services for Lincoln's funeral escort in Columbus, Ohio, 1865. Markings: PALL BEARER.

Funeral Usher's Ribbon: White silk 35½ inches long including gold tassels. Has a gold star 6 inches from bottom of silk material. Worn by Captain Watson C. Squire, 7th Independent Co., Ohio Sharpshooters, and one of "Sherman's Escort". Possibly worn at Lincoln's funeral ceremonies in Ohio, 1865.

134 PAPER HOLDER

PAPER HOLDER: Made of thin brass, 1½ inches in diameter and ⅝ of an inch deep. Marked with a eagle and **PAPER FASTENERS.** What the fasteners themselves looked like is not known since the container was empty when acquired.

PAPER HOLDER 135

Also shown here is a shield-decorated clip board type of paper fastener for use in unit headquarters. This item was used to hold the various orders and circulars emanating from higher headquarters. The clip is 4 inches tall and 2½ inches wide at the widest point. It is decorated with an eagle, stars, shield, and **E. PLURIBUS UNUM** on a scroll. The material is of thin brass, with a spring separating the front and back sections.

PARAPET BAYONET(?)

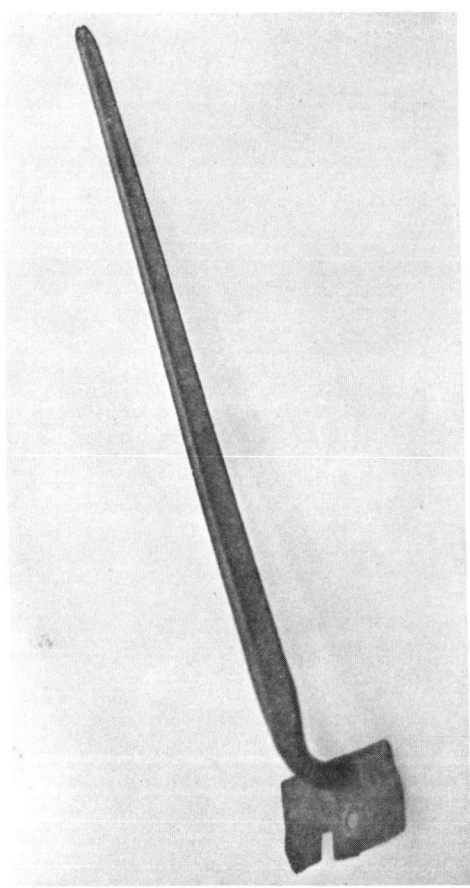

PARAPET BAYONET(?): A bayonet item of some sort — possibly for attachment to a log parapet. The bayonet proper is identical to the regulation triangular bayonet for the M. 1861 Springfield rifle musket except that the blade is only 15¼ inches long. Instead of the normal attachment section (i.e. the sleeve that slips over the barrel with a locking ring) the bayonet flares out to a flat section with a hole (possibly for a nail or screw) and an open slot. This flange section is 2½ inches by 1¾ inches in size. The item is very obviously original and made as one piece. No markings. From the battlefield of Fisher's Hill, Virginia.

PENDULUM HAUSSE 137

PENDULUM HAUSSE: Found on a battlefield — these items are rare and doubly rare when found where a battle took place. The artillery implements are rare anyway — but battlefield recovered items are extremely scarce! The artillery crews were very careful about their gun instruments! [TOM S. DICKEY; Atlanta, Georgia]

138 PERCUSSION CAP ARMLET

PERCUSSION CAP ARMLET: This is a most unique item. The leather base is 6¾ by 3¼ inches and is curved to fit the arm. Percussion caps are arranged in 5 rows with each row holding about 10 caps. This armlet was captured at Fort Donelson, Tennessee by Lieutenant H. L. BRICKETT of the 25th Indiana Infantry. The lieutenant was killed a few months later at Shiloh, April 6, 1862. [T. SHERMAN HARDING, II; Orlando, Florida]

PERCUSSION CAPS AND LOADERS 139

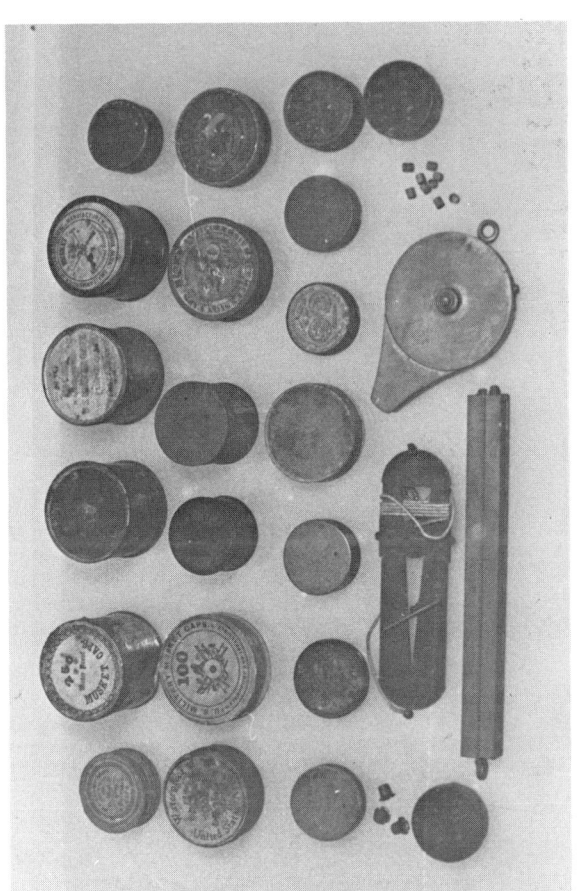

PERCUSSION CAPS AND LOADERS: Shown here are containers of both musket and pistol percussion caps. Note also the two types of percussion cap loaders and the infantry "STADIA", a device for measuring range. The long brass capper came from the Charlestown Navy Yard.

140 PEWTER CARTRIDGE BOX LINER

PEWTER CARTRIDGE BOX LINER: The Confederacy accomplished miracles in supplying its troops with the sinews of war. Here is a good example. This is a pewter cartridge box liner for holding cartridges. It is 5½ by 3½ inches and came from the battlefield of the Wilderness.

PICTURES 141

PICTURES: "A picture is worth a thousand words." This is most certainly true for our understanding of the Civil War. Through the **very** generous cooperation of RONN PALM of Monroeville, Pennsylvania, we are showing some unusually interesting pictures of Civil War soldiers. These pictures speak for themselves! [RONN PALM; Monroeville, Pennsylvania]

142 **PICTURES**

144   **PICTURES**

146 **PICTURES**

PICTURES 147

148 PICTURES

150 PICTURES

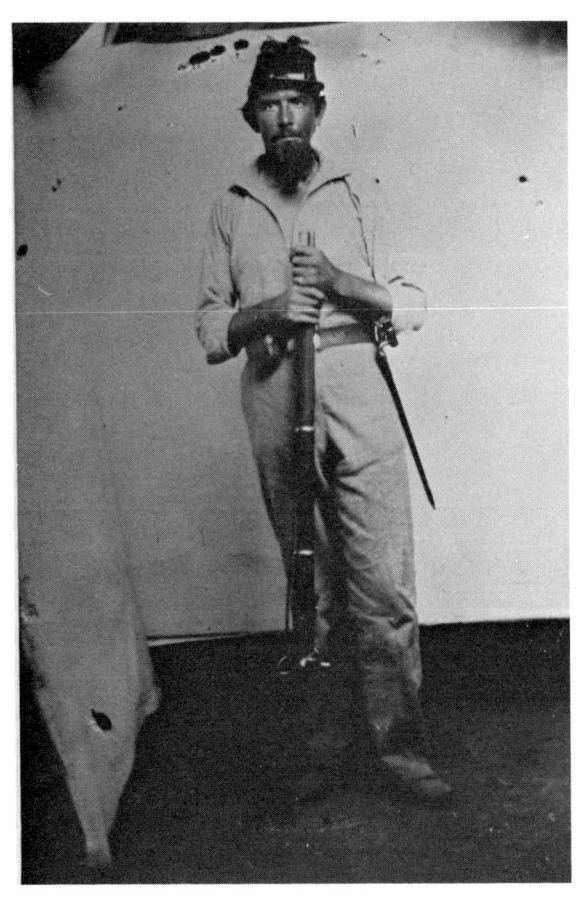

152 **PICTURES**

PICTURES 153

154   PILLS

PILLS: Concerned mothers urged their soldier sons to take pills with them to the war. Only in this way could they have protection against "swamp fever" and malaria. Shown here are two examples of the many antidotes prescribed by the soldier's relatives.

Pill Box by Herrick's Sugar Coated Pills. "Price 25 Cts." Thin wooden box is 2 inches long.

Pill Box by Sawyer's "Cholic Pills". Cost 25 cents. Box is 2⅛ inches long. Some pills are still inside!

PINFIRE AMMUNITION 155

PINFIRE AMMUNITION: Foreign pinfire revolvers were used quite extensively in the Civil War as attested to by the pinfire ammunition recovered from battlefields and camp sites. Here are two boxes of original ammunition. Both boxes are of cardboard, 4½ inches long, 1½ inches wide, and 1⅜ inches high.

    The box on the left holds 25 cartridges, caliber 12 mm, packed in sawdust. The box is marked: FABRIQUE
            DE BALLES ET CARTOUCHES
                            LEFAUCHEUX
            DE 12 MILLEMETRES

The box on the right also contains 25 cartridges. It is marked:
            CARTOUCHES
              12 MILLEMETRES
HOULLIER — BLANCHARD
ARQUEBUSIER BREVETE
      PARIS
A LONGUE PORTEE

156 PORTHOLE (C.S.N.)

PORTHOLE (C.S.N.): Rarest of the rare! A C.S. porthole recovered from a salvage dump in England. Made of very thick glass with brass rim and fixtures. **Dimensions:** A diameter of 19½ inches overall with the glass diameter of 13½ inches. **Markings:** C.S.S. COTTON.

POSTER: In the days before radio and television and when even newspapers were rare in some rural areas, the poster was used extensively to disseminate news. At times, these posters departed from their usual norm of "straight reporting" and were couched in humorous lines. Here is such a poster — announcing a Fourth of July program in Connecticut. It was written before the North was aware of the long, costly war ahead of it. **Dimensions:** 23⅞ inches tall and 8½ inches wide. Only about 2 weeks after this celebration, 3 Connecticut regiments fought at First Bull Run. Many of the men came from Meriden, Connecticut — locale of the July 4th celebration.

158 POWDER CANS

POWDER CANS: Although most ammunition in the Civil War was "fixed", i.e. already prepared for use in weapons by both sides, some powder was used — either from large containers like metal or wood barrels, or from smaller cans as shown here. In fact, a surprisingly large number of cans like these have been recovered from battlefield and camp sites.

The large can is 4½ inches tall, 4½ inches wide, and 2 inches deep. it is of tin, painted black. The paper label says: -CKY RIFLE GUNPOWDER
  HAZARD POWDER CO.

The small can is of japanned tin, 3⅛ inches tall, 2¾ inches wide, and 1⅛ inches deep. There are no markings on the metal of the can, but the old paper label says: MADE "FOR SMALL PISTOLS".

PROJECTILES 159

PROJECTILES: This is definitely one of the very best collections of Civil War projectiles in existence. Not only are the main types here but many rare types as well. Only an extremely dedicated and knowledgeable expert could have assembled so fine a collection as this. It is truly fantastic! [TOM S. DICKEY; Atlanta, Georgia]

RAILROAD ITEMS

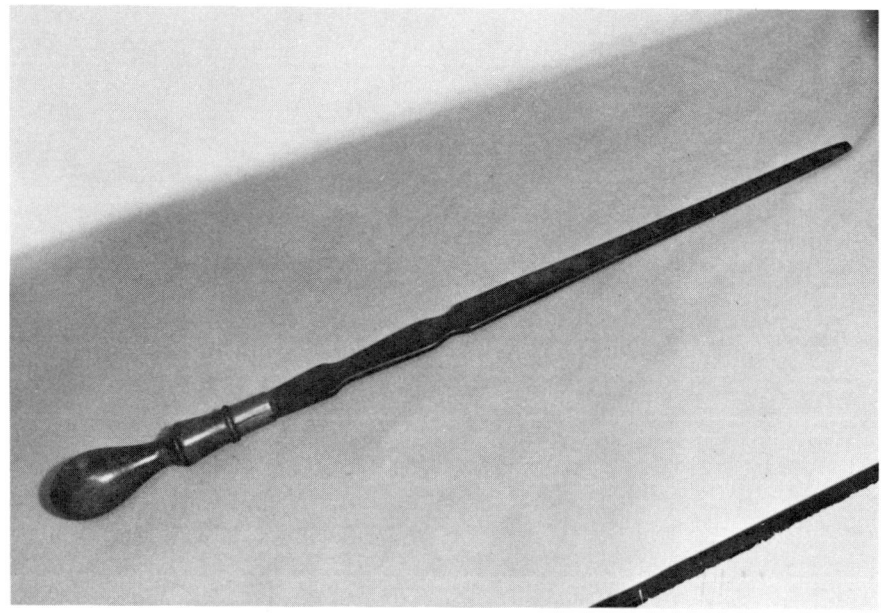

RAILROAD ITEMS: One of the baffling mysteries of Civil War collecting is whatever happened to all the railroad items used. We know that railroads were very extensively used by both sides. Yet railroad items which definitely were used **during the war** are rare indeed. Shown here are some examples:

Screwdriver (Railroad): Steel screwdriver with wooden handle. Overall length is 24½ inches; the blade is 18 inches long. Used during the Gettysburg campaign on the Western Maryland Railroad by locomotive engineer John Nelson Hymiller. (See data on this railroad in author's *Herman Haupt: Lincoln's Railroad Man.*) **No markings.**

Oil Can (Railroad): For steam locomotive. Made of brass with an overall length of 23 inches. The spout is 17 inches long; diameter of the can is 4 inches. **No markings.**

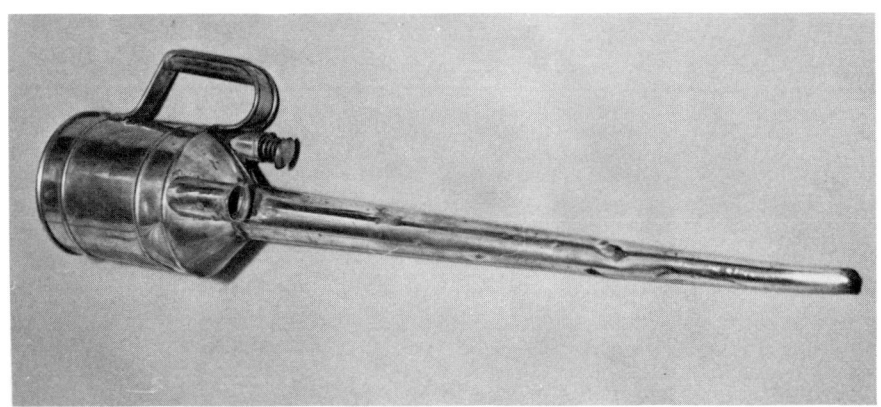

RAIL

Rail: Section of iron "strap rail" from a C.S. camp at Nickerjack Cove (north of Chattanooga). This rail is 2½ inches wide with 14 inches between holes where the rail was fastened to the "stringers".

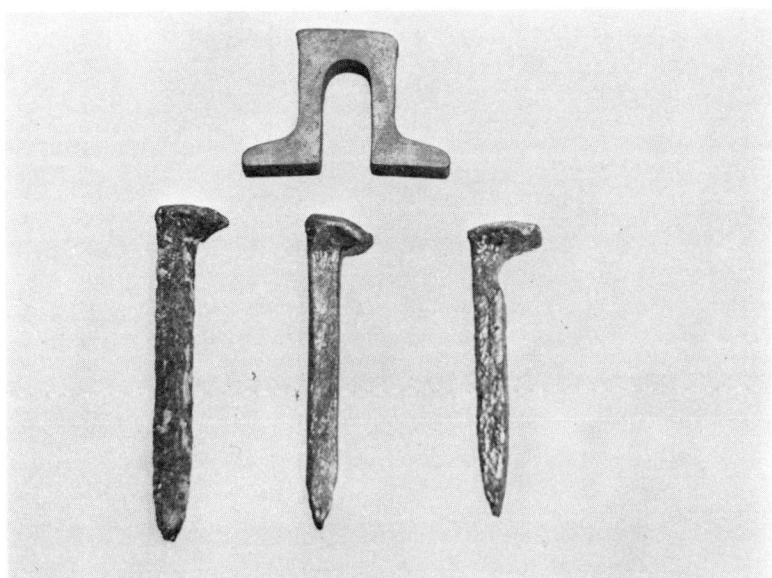

Miscellaneous Railroad Items: Three spikes: Left to Right: The longest is 6 inches in length and was found in a fort on the **Orange and Alexandria Railroad** (Virginia). The second longest is 5½ inches in length and came off the sunken Federal ship CAIRO. The shortest is 5⅛ inches long. Note the wear under the head of this spike — the wear being made by the flange of the rail. From the **Memphis and Charleston Railroad** at LaGrange, Tennessee. With this spike was found a U.S. eagle "I" button.

Also shown is a cross-section of a rail from Ezra Church, Georgia. This section is 2¾ inches tall and 3⅞ inches wide at the bottom.

162 RAINCOAT

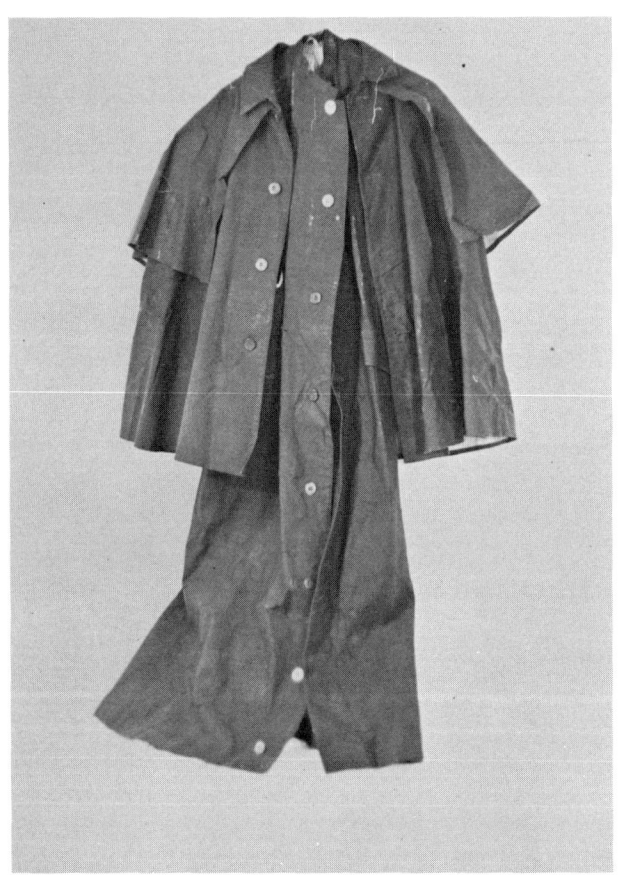

RAINCOAT: An interesting raincoat because it differs markedly from the more common rubber coat. This raincoat is light blue in color and made of a water-proofed canvas material. The cape is detachable. Worn early in the war by Lyman Stowe of the 2nd Michigan Infantry.

RED TAPE   163

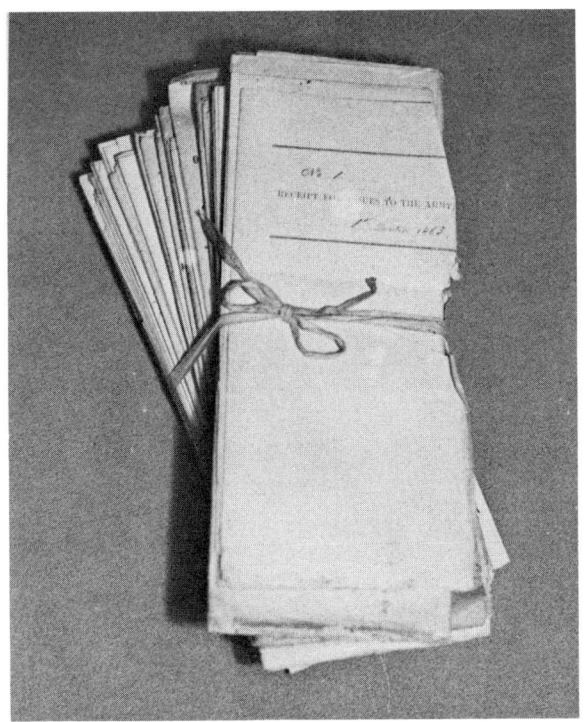

RED TAPE: The term "red tape" has a definite — and really negative — connotation in American military parlance. There was a great deal of red tape in our Civil War — literally! Shown here is a photograph of documents enclosed by a cloth strip which is definitely **RED**. These documents are all dated in 1863 and have not been untied since that time. They came from the field desk of Colonel J. B. McCown of the 63rd Illinois Infantry and were issued during the Vicksburg campaign.

RELIGIOUS MEDAL: Thin medal — "Immaculate Heart of Mary" found in Sherman's lines, siege of Savannah. Only 1 inch long and ¾ of an inch wide. Is decorated with religious symbols of the Roman Catholic Faith.

164 REVOLVER

REVOLVER: Here is one of those "unique" weapons imported from Europe in the early months of the war. It is a caliber .44 LaFaucheux revolver with a folding bayonet 4¾ inches long. This weapon is 6-shots and 12 inches in length. The lettering on top of the barrel is illegible. The weapon came from Nashville, Tennessee.

RIFLES AND MUSKETS: Various long arms are constantly turning up that are of interest to the Civil War student and collector. Shown here are four:

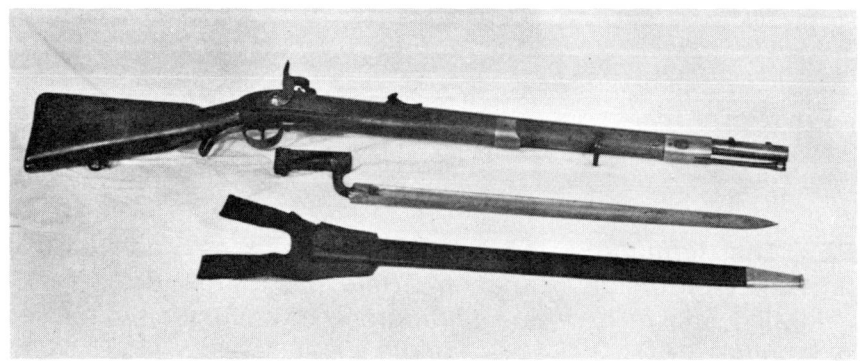

Ohio Rifle Musket: Heavy octagonal barrel, with brass bands. Caliber .58. Length overall is 43½ inches with a 28 inch barrel. Has a cheekpiece. Equipped with a sword bayonet 28 inches long with a 23½ inch blade. The black leather scabbard is stamped: OHIO. **Markings:** On the top of barrel — SEDERL; on lock plate — (1)861.

HUNTING RIFLE 165

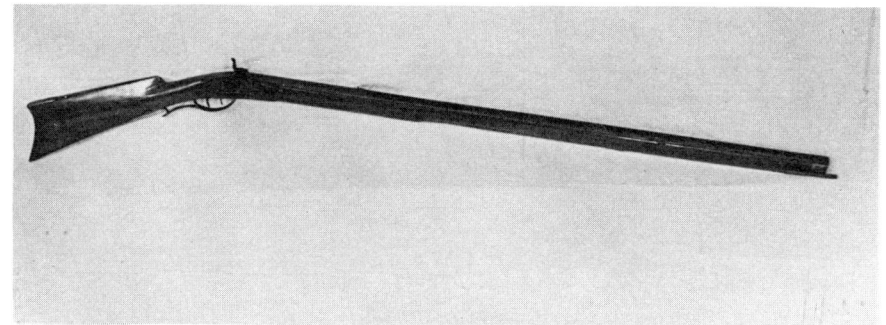

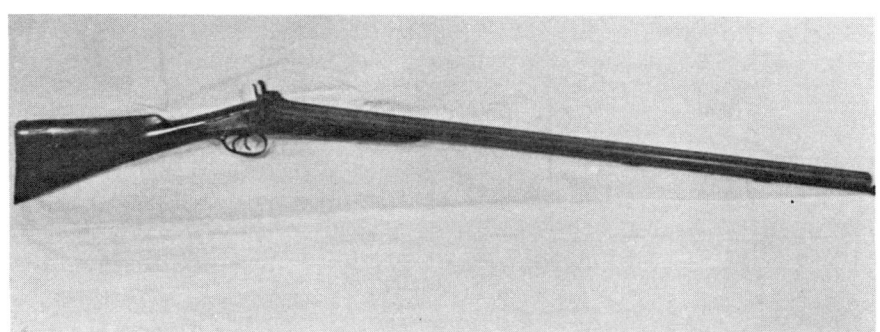

Hunting Rifle: Used by a C.S. volunteer in 1861. Length 58 inches with a 41 inch barrel. Heavy octagonal barrel with brass furniture throughout. Caliber — about .36. Wood ramrod. **Markings:** On lock plate — A. W. SPIES. Spies made rifles in New York during the period 1820-1851.

Shotgun: Used by a South Carolina cavalryman, it is 52½ inches long; each barrel is 36½ inches long. 12-gauge. Steel ramrod. **Markings:** J. MANTON. Joseph Manton of London made this shotgun about 1850.

166 C.S. MUSKETOON

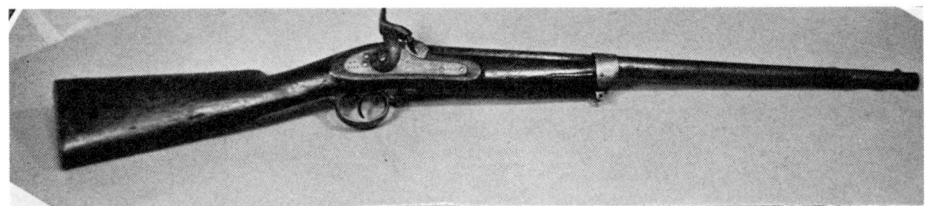

C.S. Musketoon: This weapon is very probably C.S. made but complete identification has not yet been made. It is 39 inches long with a 24-inch barrel. There is a stud for a sword bayonet. Brass furniture. The weapon is of the Enfield type but is caliber .58. **Markings:** (On lockplate) A E
                                     1864
The lettering is crude.

SABER BOX 167

SABER BOX: Very similar to the musket box as described on page 116 in this volume. Made of plain pine, 4 feet 5½ inches long; 19½ inches wide, and 14¼ inches deep (including the cover). **Markings:**

          30
CAVALRY SABRES
HEAVY AM.
SMALL GRIP — FLAT BACK
AMES   1st CLASS
AGH

168 SADDLE CLOTH

SADDLE CLOTH: Worn under the saddle by officers, generally of field grade or higher. Very finely made — very expensive — and today, very rare! This particular saddle cloth was for a major general as can be seen by the two stars. Made of blue woolen cloth and trimmed with gold-colored bands. It is leather-reinforced with slots for the stirrups straps. Length — 3 feet at longest point; width 21½ inches on each side.

SASH   169

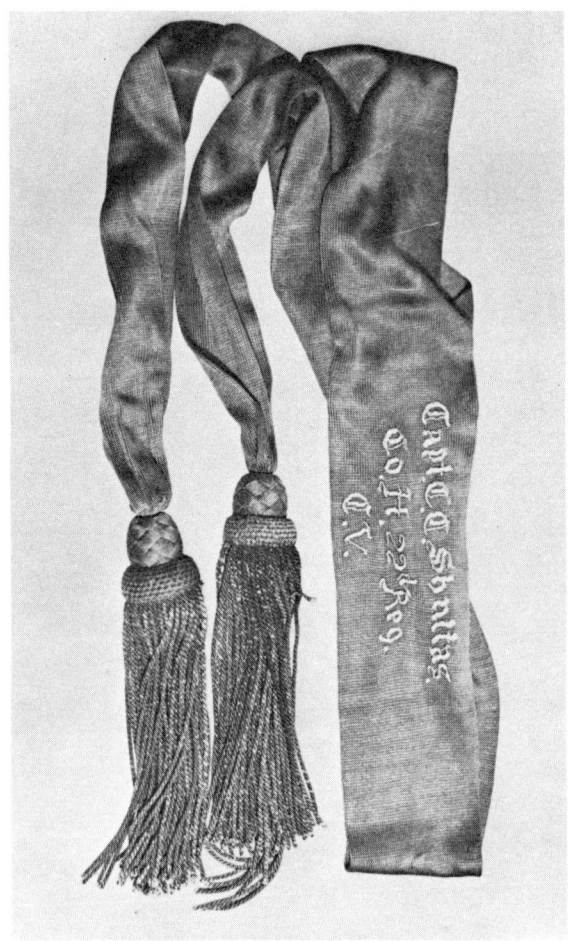

SASH: Officer's red silk sash, about 9 feet long, and 3⅝ inches wide at the middle and tapering to the tassels. Beautifully stitched on this sash (probably by wife or sweetheart!) is: CAPT. C. C. SHULTAS
        CO. H 22d REG.
        C.V.

The 22nd Connecticut Infantry was a nine-month's unit.

170 SECRETARY

SECRETARY: A fine homemade, crocheted pocket secretary. It is 8 inches long when closed; open it is 8 by 8 inches. White on the outside and bright red on the inside. Was carried in the war by Captain A. H. ALEXANDER, Co. "A" 103rd Pennsylvania Infantry. [ARTHUR LEE BREWER, JR.; Durham, North Carolina]

SECRETARY 171

SHARPSHOOTER'S GLASSES

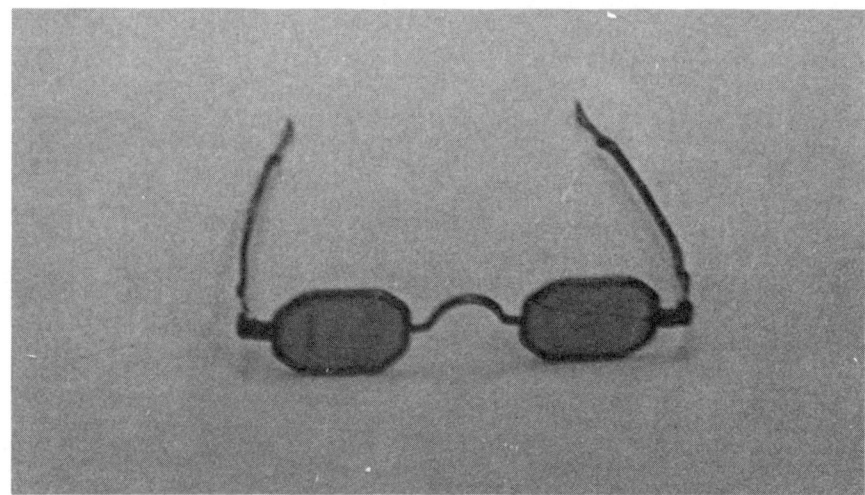

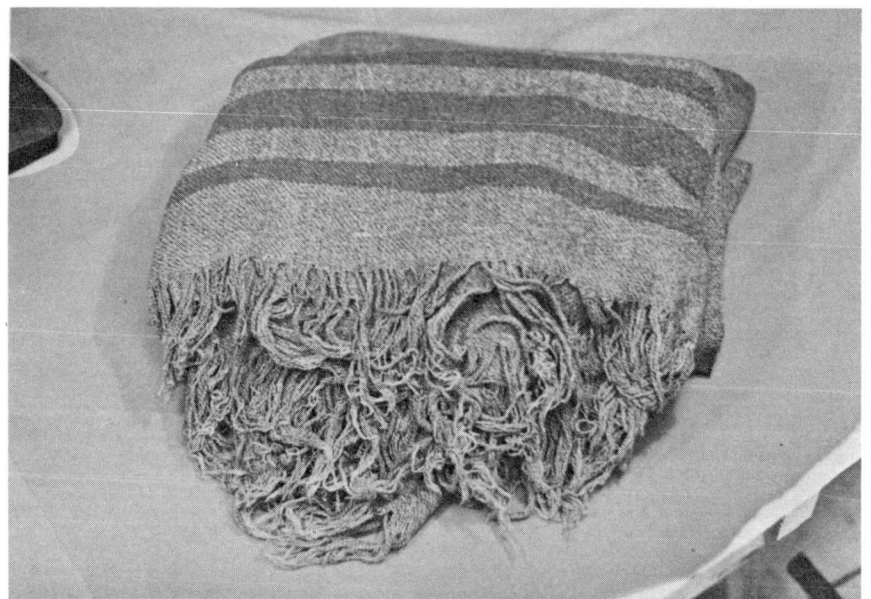

SHARPSHOOTER'S GLASSES: Glasses made especially for a sharpshooter. Note the circular clear lens on the right glass. The glasses themselves have dark glass except for the lighter circular lens which is barely perceptible in the photograph. Frames are of brass and are adjustable. These glasses only saw limited use in the field but apparently were used some. [BILL HOWARD; Delmar, New York]

SHAWL: This luxury certainly was not used at the front very long! It is a 10 by 5 foot shawl made of beautifully pure wool. There is a fringe on both ends. Used in the war by First Lieutenant WILLIAM S. AMES of the 38th U.S. Colored Troops. **No markings.**

SHELTER HALF 173

SHELTER HALF: Although shelter tents were used by the thousands during the war, this specimen is one of the few authenticated examples known to exist today.

Dimensions: 64 inches by 64 inches. All four corners are reinforced with 4 inches by 5 inches pieces of canvas. There is a total of 31 button holes. This specimen is made of canvas. Used by NATHAN RUSSELL, Co. "F" 38th Massachusetts Infantry.

Markings: In an oval shield — JOSEPH LEE
64 & 66
Lispenard &
62 Walker Sts.
New York

[From the collection of WILLIAM C. McKENNA, Westmont, N.J. Photographs by STEVEN MILLER, Audobon, N.J.]

174 SHOT LADLE

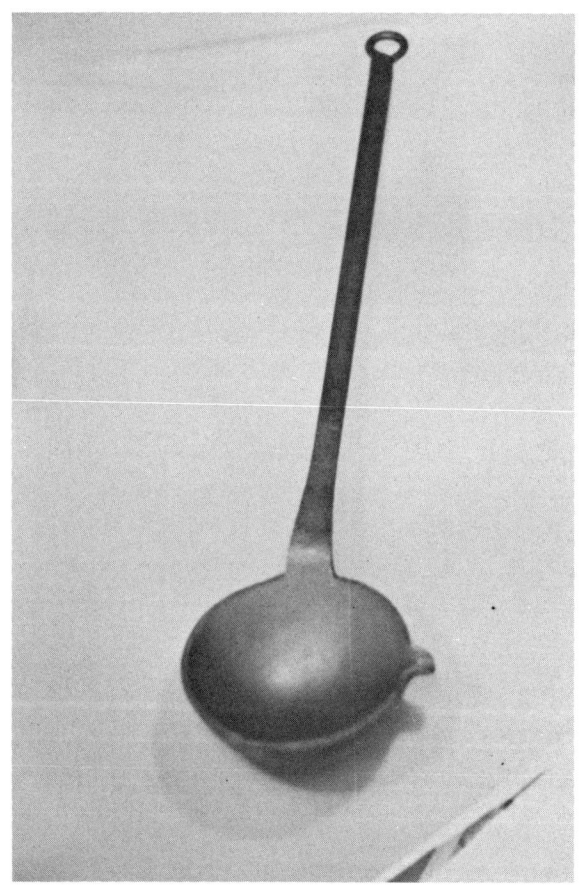

SHOT LADLE: Iron shot ladle weighing about 5 pounds with an overall length of 31 inches. The bowl is 6⅞ inches in diameter and 3 inches deep. **No markings.**

Also shown is a shot-making outfit — probably Confederate. This came from Lancaster, South Carolina. **No markings.**

SHOT LADLE 175

176 SHOULDER KNOTS

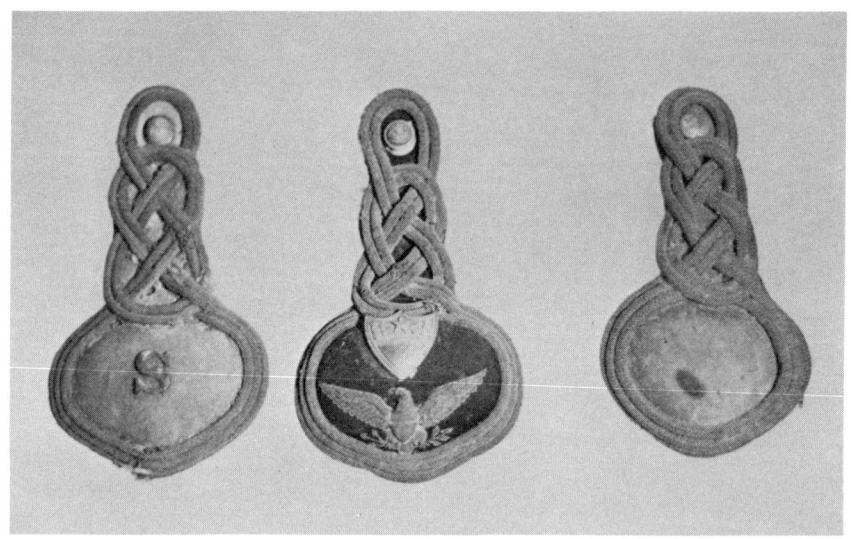

SHOULDER KNOTS: Although this type of shoulder insignia was to become very popular in the post-Civil War era, some officers did wear the shoulder knot during the 1861-1865 period. The three examples shown here were worn during the Civil War.

Left to Right:

Marked **S.** Gray with red and blue cording and a New York State button.

Colonel's shoulder knot with a silver shield decorated with stars. The cloth is dark blue with gray cording, and a U.S. staff officer's button. **Markings:** HARTLEY & GRAHAM
 NEW YORK

Red shoulder knot with green cording. The button has a harp motif. Worn by an Irish regiment — the 69th New York Infantry.

SOUVENIRS 177

SOUVENIRS:

Wooden Plaque: Plaque made from a hardtack box on which is fastened some battlefield bullets and other relics from the 1864 siege of Petersburg. The long piece of wood at the top is marked: PIECE OF CHEVEAUX DE FRISE
FROM REBEL FORT "MAHONE"
CALLED BY THE SOLDIERS
FORT DAMNATION!

The round piece of wood is marked: SABOT
3-INCH CANISTER
FROM REBEL FORT MAHONE
PROBABLY FIRED _____

The piece of wood at bottom of the plaque is marked:

PIECE OF "BOMB PROOF"
FROM FORT SEDGWICK,
CALLED BY THE SOLDIERS
FORT HELL!

178   BRICK

Brick: Complete brick 8½ by 4 by 1¾ inches. Marked: CANNON DESIGN
and MALVERN HILL
JULY 1st 1862

Small piece of brick: taken from the Dunkard Church at Antietam. **Dimensions:** 1 inch square and 3¾ inches long.

Piece of wood from the Andersonville Prison stockade. Dimensions: 1 inch square and 2⅝ inches long. A label on the wood reads: SOLD BY A MEMBER OF
THE GAR WHO GOT IT
WHILE ASST. ADJ. GEN. OF
THE DEPT. OF GEORGIA.
36th ANNUAL ENCAMPMENT GAR

BULLETS IN MEDICINE BOTTLE   179

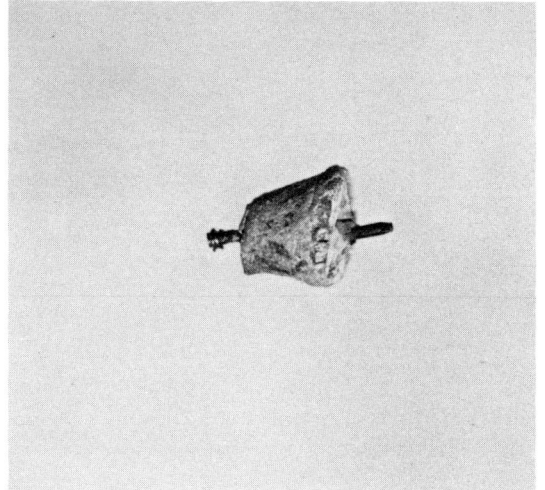
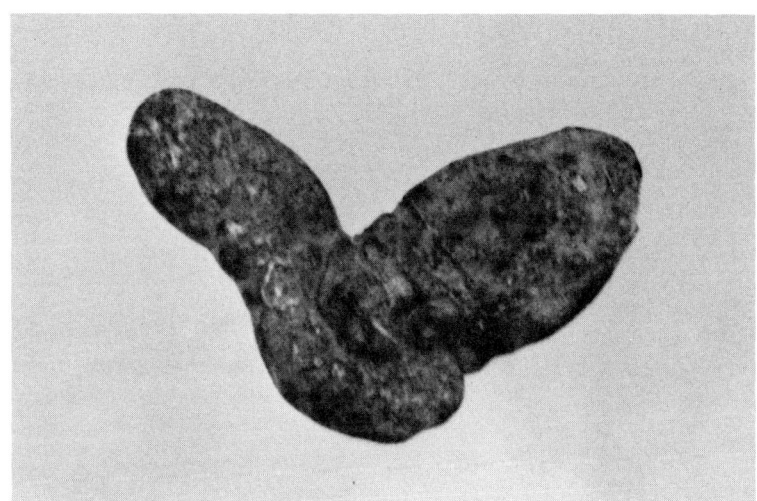

Bullets in Medicine Bottle: This bottle contains 2 bullets taken from a wounded soldier. He was PETER S. CHASE, Co. "I", 2nd Vermont Infantry. CHASE was wounded twice — at Fredericksburg (Dec. 13, 1862) and at the Wilderness (May 5, 1864). The two bullets were taken from his leg after Fredericksburg. The label on top of the bottle gives the information cited above. The medicine bottle is 3 inches tall and 1¾ inches in diameter. Chase died September 16, 1927.

Extracted Bullet: Bullet extracted from leg of a Federal soldier by Assistant Surgeon ROBERT W. ELMER, 23rd New Jersey Infantry. The soldier's name and battle are not recorded. The bullet fragment has a nail in it (probably used to put up on display); the bullet itself is caliber .44.

Bullets That Met in Mid-air: ARTHUR LEE BREWER, JR. of Durham, North Carolina contributes this photo of two bullets which met in mid-air at Gettysburg.

180 SPIGOTS

SPIGOTS: Pewter spigots from barrels used in the field. The top spigot came from an Alabama camp at Dumfries, Virginia. **Markings:** NEW YORK
NO. 3

The bottom spigot top came from a campsite at Eastport, Mississippi. **No markings.**

 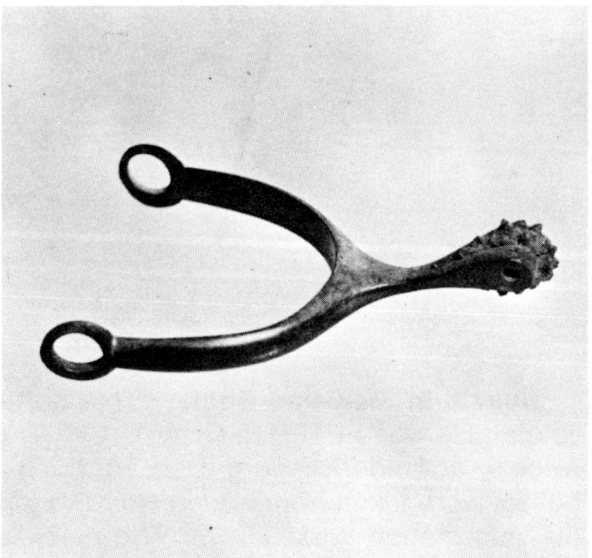

SPURS: Shown here are contrasting types of spurs. The Federal spur (with the spur strap) is of ornately decorated brass. It is of regulation size and shape. There are 6 stars on each side of the spur with **U.S.** in block letters separated by a large star just over the rowel projection. [RONN PALM; Monroeville, Pennsylvania]

The C.S. spur is made of brass. Its total length is 5¼ inches and came from the 1861 battle at Dranesville, Virginia.

STATE DOCUMENTS

STATE DOCUMENTS: The collecting of Civil War documents is, of course, a field in itself. The three shown here are self-explanatory. These colorful items were highly prized and were hung with pride in the family livingroom. [TOM MacDONALD; Eustis, Maine]

STATE DOCUMENTS

STATE DOCUMENTS 183

184 STRETCHER

STRETCHER: A heavy stretcher used in the field. It is 8 feet 2 inches long, about 2¾ feet wide, equipped with a thin canvas material of which only fragments remain. This stretcher was used at the battle of ANTIETAM, September 17, 1862.

SUSPENDERS 185

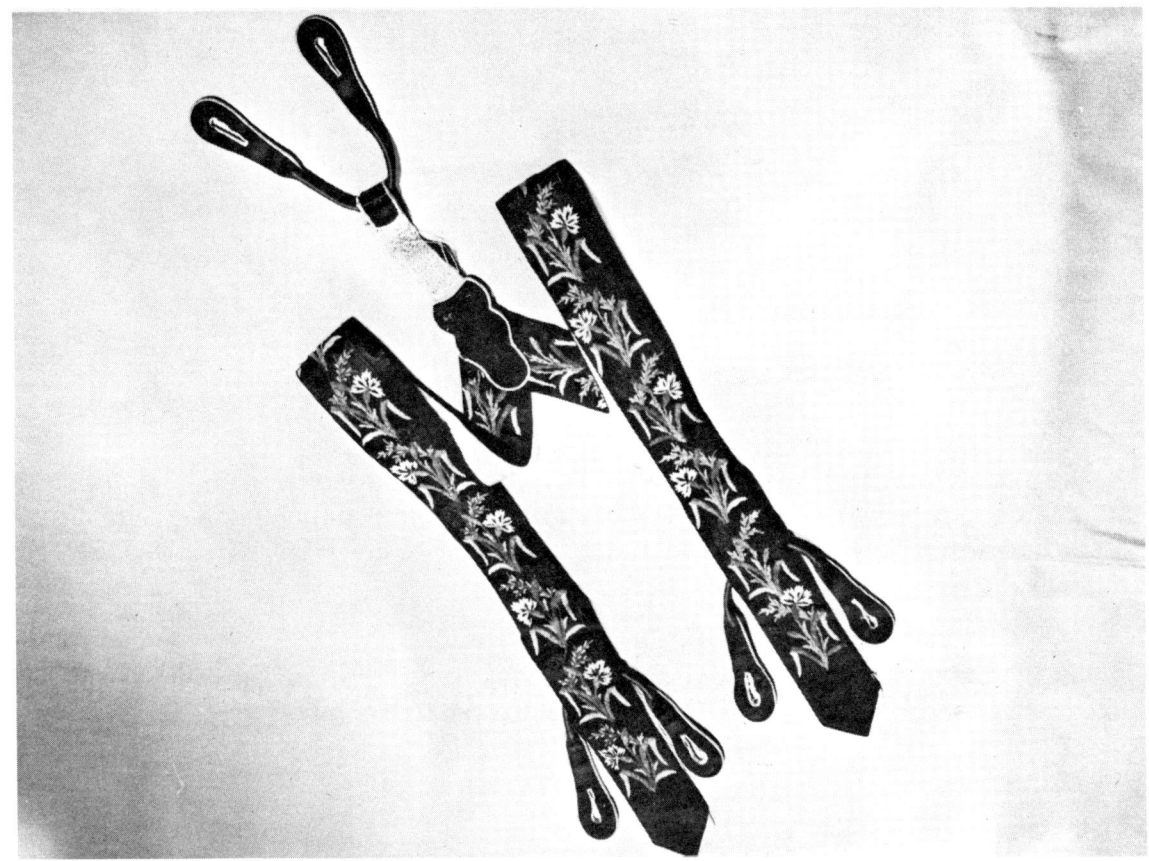

SUSPENDERS: Civil War soldiers used suspenders, **not** belts to hold up their trousers. Many did not even wear suspenders; they merely buttoned their trousers tight enough to keep the trousers up around their waists. I have never even seen a pair of Civil War suspenders; they are rare! But here are photographs of a pair worn by GEORGE W. BARNES, Co. "H", 36th Massachusetts Infantry. The cloth of these suspenders is 1⅝ inches wide. The clips are the same type as shown on page 188 of Vol. II of the *Encyclopedia*. [ROBERT CORRETTE; Fitzwilliam, New Hampshire]

186 TASSEL FOR HOSPITAL PATIENT

TASSEL FOR HOSPITAL PATIENT: A yellow wool tassel worn by patients in U.S. military hospitals. Total length 6¾ inches. The original paper package holding this tassel had the following written in faded ink: WORN BY HOSPITAL PATIENTS ON UNIFORM.

TELEGRAPH KEY: Thin brass, 2⅜ inches long. Found at Civil War site on Polegreen Road, Hanover County, Virginia in 1962. **No markings.**

TENT ROPE TIGHTENERS

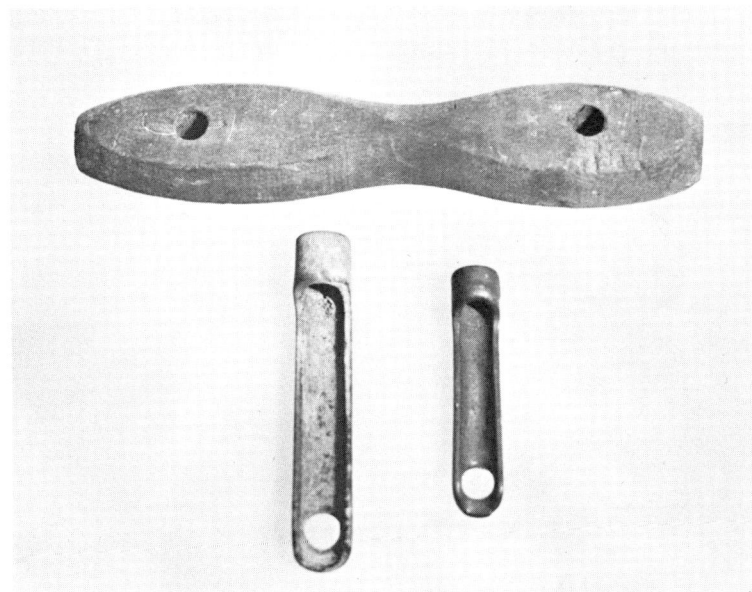

TENT ROPE TIGHTENERS: Apparently there has been little change in the basic types of tent rope tighteners since 1865. The three shown here are from the Civil War. The large wooden specimen is 8 inches long, 1½ inches wide at widest point, and 1 inch thick. It is made of hard pine.

The larger of the metal specimens is of heavy brass, 4 inches long. It came from Cold Harbor. The smaller specimen is also of heavy brass, but is only 3 inches long.

TOILET ARTICLES:
Toilet Kit: Made of heavy black cardboard with a small lock. Kit is 7 inches tall, 5⅝ inches wide, 3½ inches deep. A very elegant outfit. Included in the contents are various

188 TOOTH BRUSHES

brushes, shaving items, mirror, a pearl handle bottle opener, large needle, pearl handle shears, steel boot hooks, a bottle. **Markings:** J. B. WILLIAMS CO.
MUG
SHAVING
SOAP

Used during the war by a soldier from Carmel, Maine.

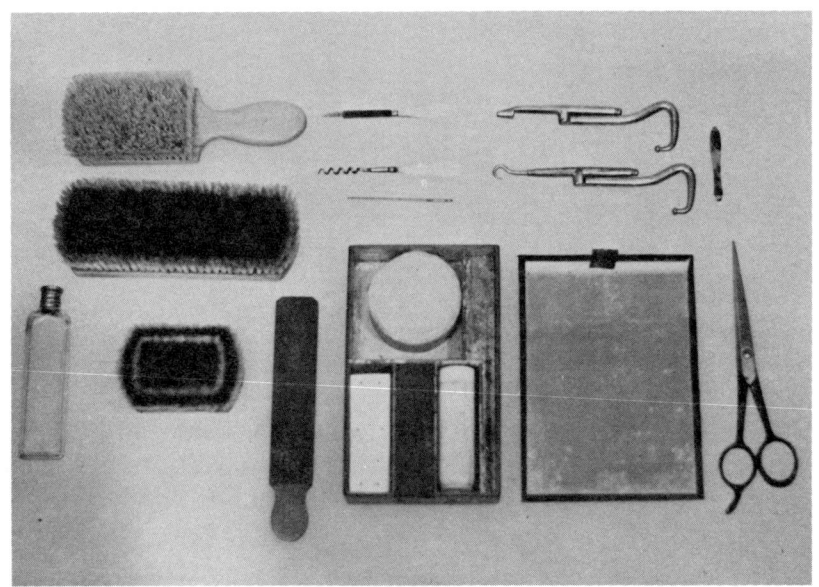

Tooth Brushes:

Top: Bone handle, 6½ inches long. **Markings:** EXTRA FINE PARIS FRANCE. Used by W. L. Ames, 117th New York Infantry.

Bottom: Bone handle, 6½ inches long. **Markings:** STURTEVANT'S SPECIAL NO. 45, FRANCE. Used by Surgeon ENOCH PEARCE, 61st Ohio Infantry.

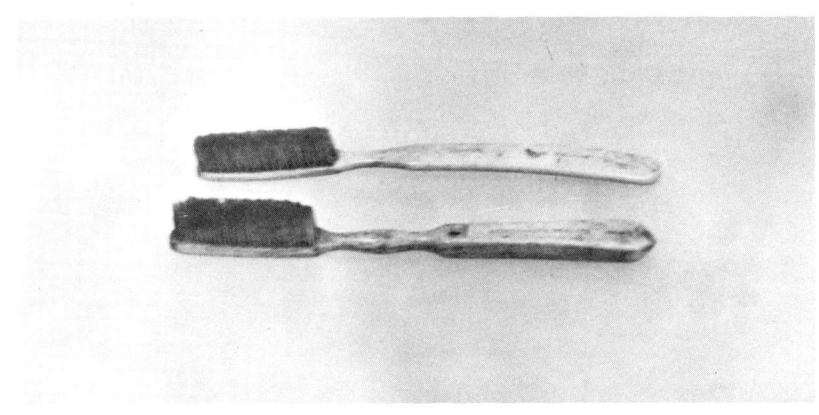

TOILETRY BOTTLES 189

Toiletry Bottles: Left to Right
1) Clear glass, 6⅛ inches tall. **Markings:** TRICOPHEROUS
FOR THE SKIN AND HAIR
NEW YORK
BARRY'S
2) Clear glass, 5⅞ inches tall. **Markings:** LYON'S
NEW YORK
KATHAIRON
FOR THE HAIR
3) Brown glass, 4⅞ inches tall. **Markings:** BUCKINGHAM
WHISKER DYE

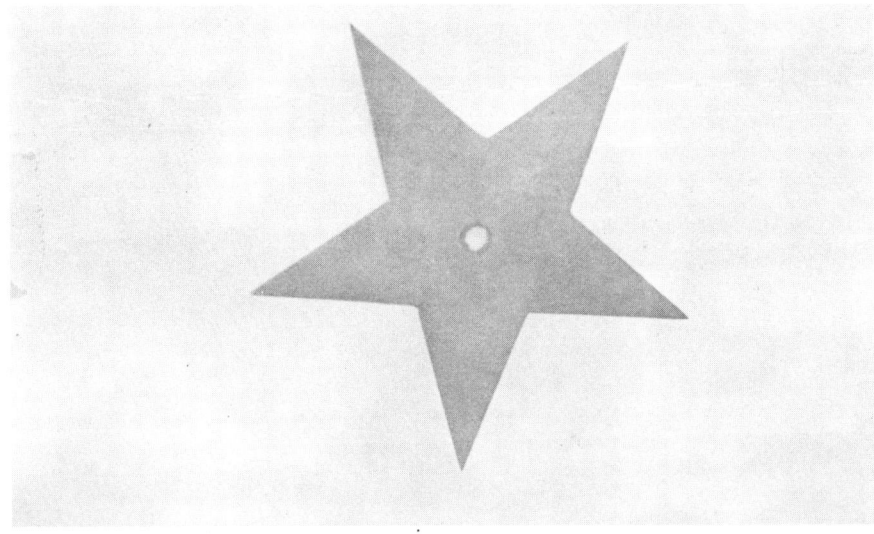

TOMPION STAR: Made of medium heavy brass. Greatest width — 6¼ inches. From the tompion of a large naval cannon.

190 TOMPIONS

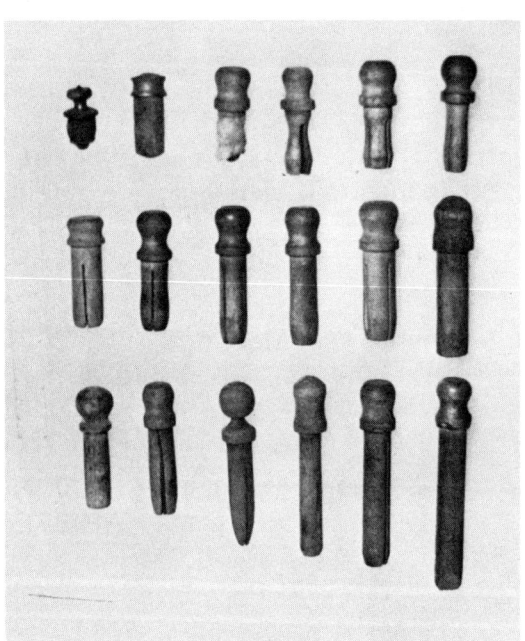

TOMPIONS: The tompion was a wooden or cork plug inserted into the muzzle of a gun to keep out water, dirt, etc. Shown here are 18 different types and calibers. All were used during the war.

TOOTH EXTRACTOR   191

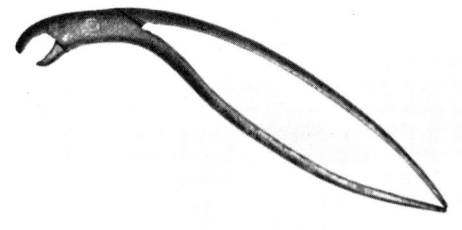

TOOTH EXTRACTOR: Crude iron extractor found in the CHINN HOUSE on the battlefield of FIRST BULL RUN (FIRST MANASSAS). This extractor was found in the rafters of the CHINN HOUSE which served as a hospital. Total length 6¼ inches. **No markings.**

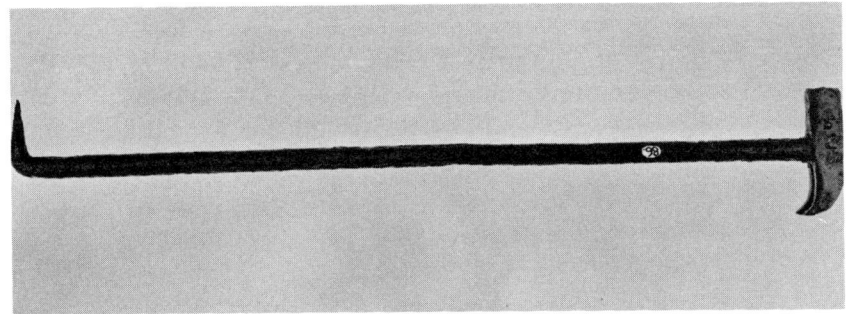

TOW HOOK: This is an artillery implement used for unpacking ammunition chests. The one shown here is 14⅞ inches long. Length of the hammer head is 2 inches. From the battlefield of SHILOH. [TOM DICKEY; Atlanta, Georgia]

VETERAN RESERVE CORPS BELT

VETERAN RESERVE CORPS BELT: Beautiful buff leather belt for noncomissioned officers of the Veteran Reserve Corps. The belt is 36¾ inches long, 1¾ inches wide, excluding the buckle. **Markings:** (on inside of the belt) HERMAN OTTO
Co. H 17 r
2nd V.R.C.

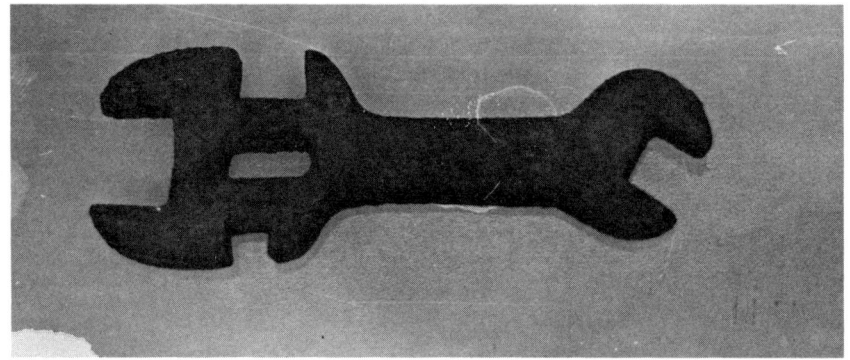

WAGON WRENCH: Very unusual iron wrench for use by army teamsters on their wagons. Overall length 7¾ inches. Width at widest place is 2¾ inches. This wrench is ⅝ of an inch thick! No markings. From Falmouth, Virginia camp of the Army of the Potomac.

WAR LOG 193

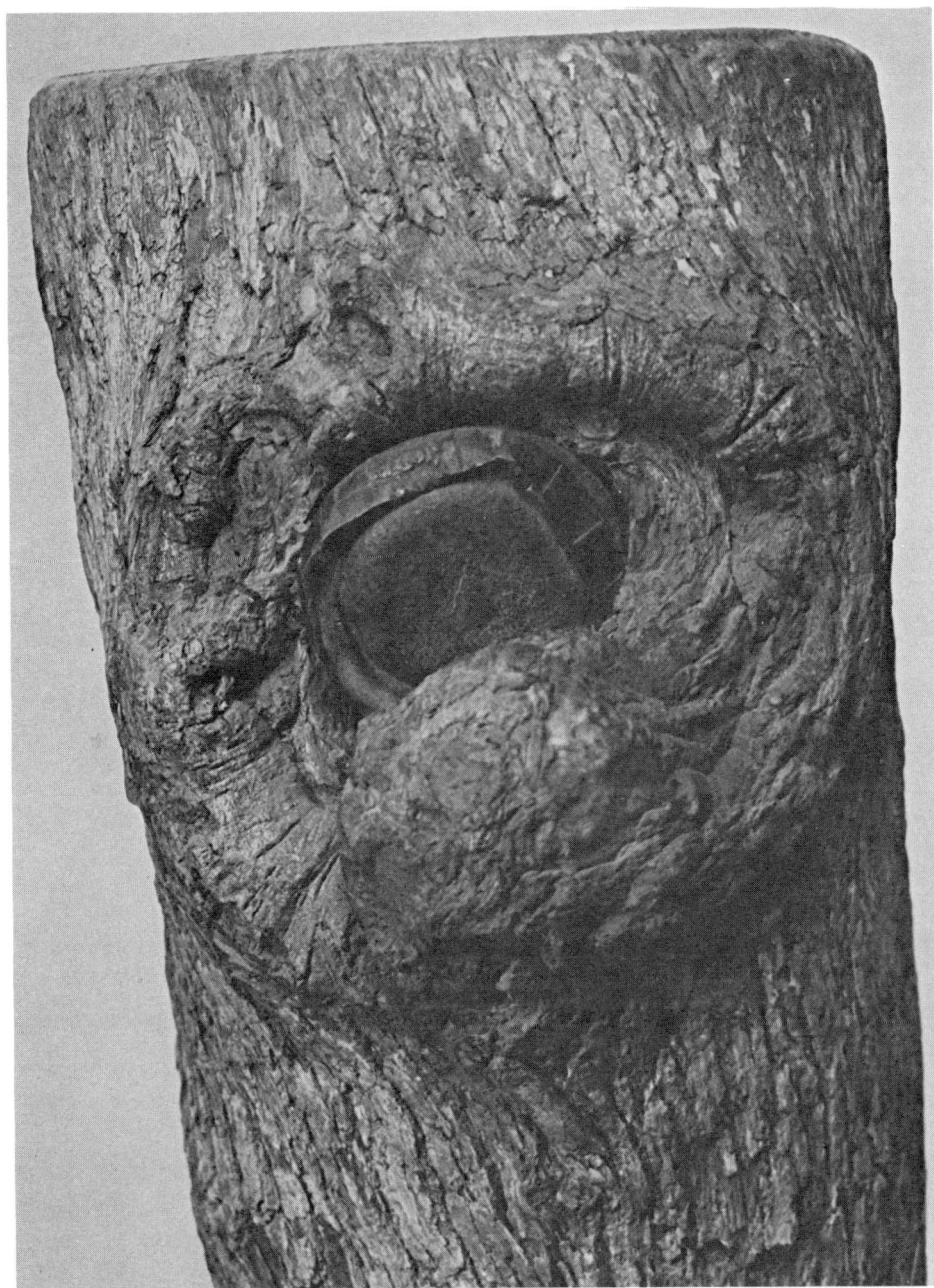

WAR LOG: Shown here are three "war logs" from Western Theater battlefields. As can be seen from the photographs, the term "war log" applies to a section of a tree which has a projectile in it. For many years after the war the "war log" was a prized souvenir. But all too often the wood rotted away and eventually only the projectile was left. However, here are three excellent "souvenirs".

No. 1: Oak log with the base end showing of a C.S. 3.8-inch Reed shell. Probably from CHICKAMAUGA.

194 WAR LOG

No. 2: Pine log with a C.S. 3-inch Archer projectile imbedded in it. From CHICKAMAUGA.

WAR LOG 195

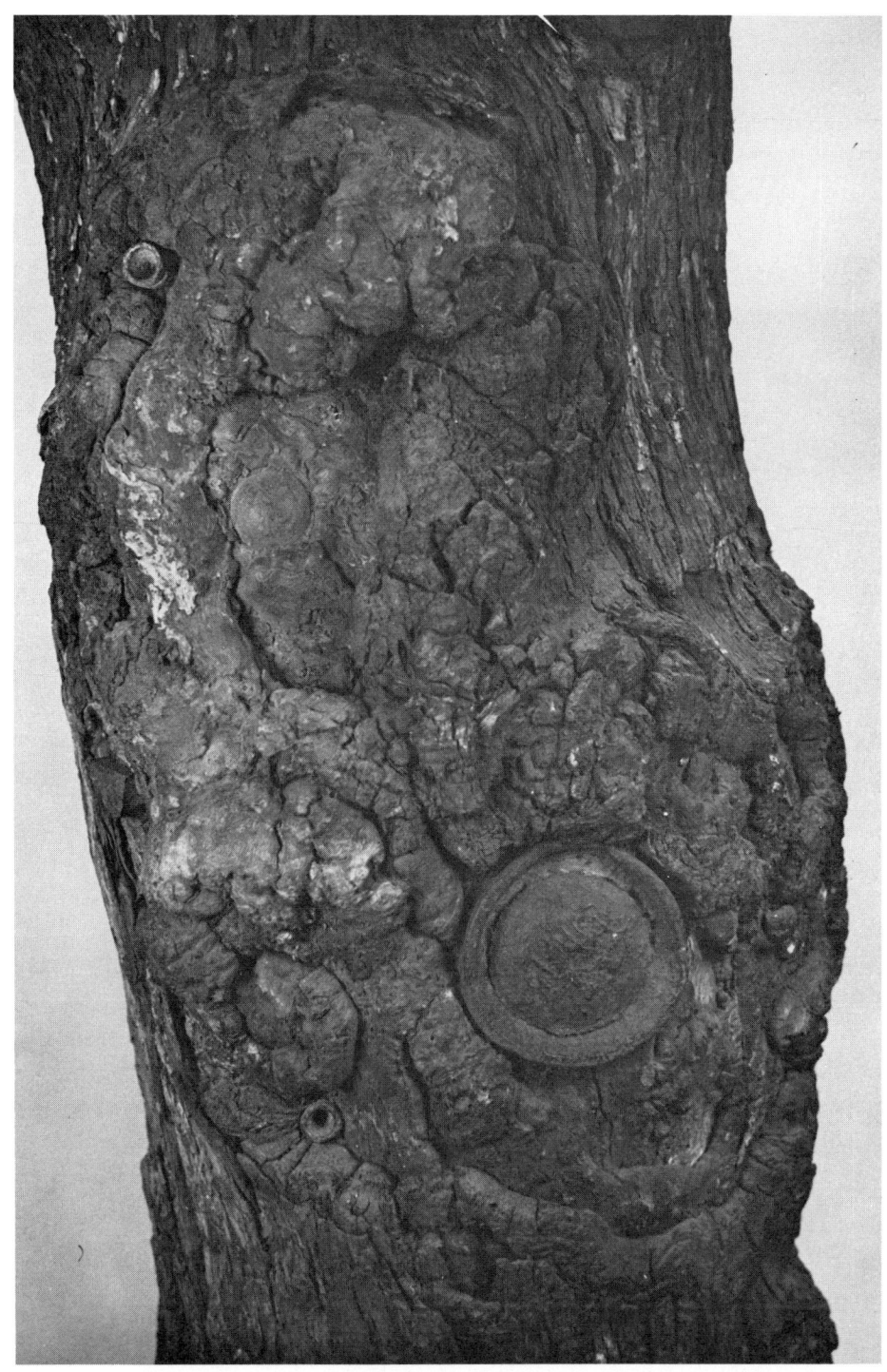

No. 3: This log has a 10-pounder Parrott shell and 2 bullets plus an iron canister shot imbedded in it. (For the bullets and iron canister shot — look to the left of the picture.) From KENNESAW MOUNTAIN, Georgia. [TOM DICKEY; Atlanta, Georgia]

196 WATER FILTER CANTEENS

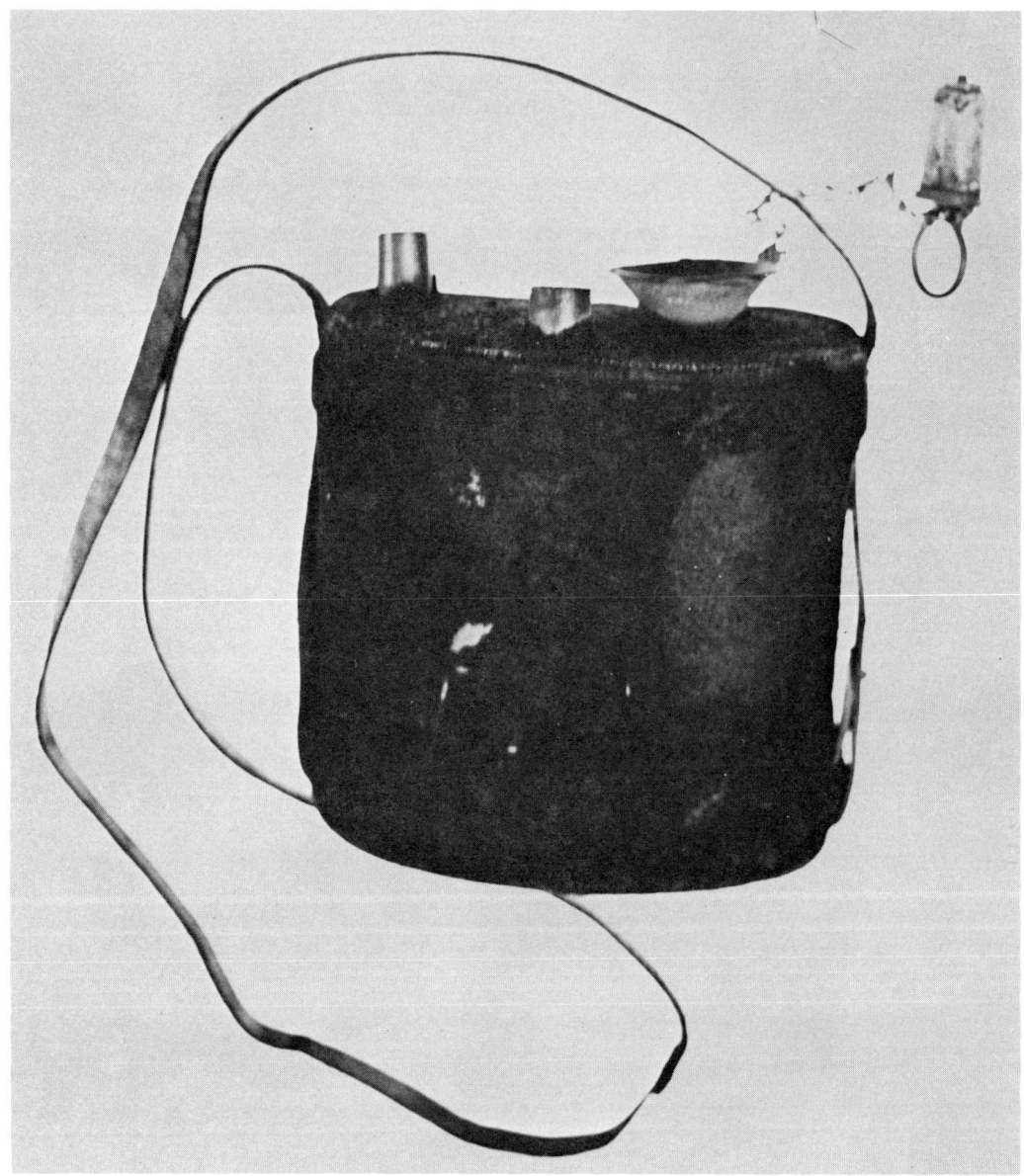

WATER FILTER CANTEENS: Since most roads of the 1861-1865 period were unpaved, mud and dust were often very much in evidence for soldiers as they moved around camp or on the march. Because of the mud and dust the soldiers had difficulty in finding clear drinking water. Accordingly, especially in 1861, some soldiers carried the "water filter" canteen. Shown here are two types.

3-spout: Has a blue wool cover. This canteen is 6¼ inches tall and 6¼ inches wide. **No markings.** [ARTHUR LEE BREWER, JR.; Durham, North Carolina]

2-SPOUT 197

2-spout: This specimen is very probably Confederate. It is 6¼ inches tall and 6¾ inches wide. **No markings.** [ARTHUR LEE BREWER, JR.; Durham, North Carolina]

198 WEDGE

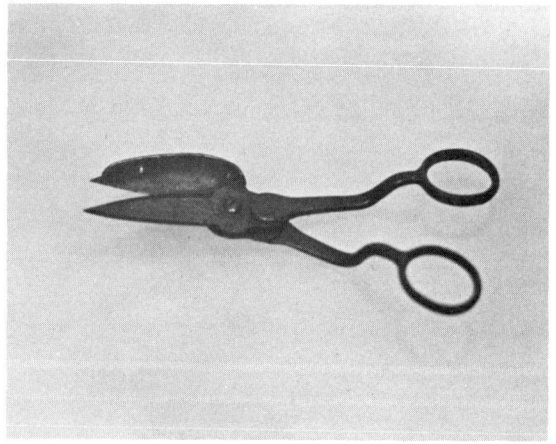

WEDGE: Shown here are three excavated items from the site of the Federal FORT MACGILVRAY at PETERSBURG. Of especial interest is the splitting wedge shown in the center of the picture. This type of wedge was used in splitting logs for construction of huts or for use on the fortifications.

WHISTLE: Whistles and any reference to their use during the Civil War are very rare. This pewter whistle dug up at Port Hudson was probably used by an officer. Length 1¼ inches, with a diameter of ¾ of an inch. **No markings.**

WICK CUTTER: Used with candles. This specimen is made of good steel, 5¾ inches long. **Markings:** W. B. BARNARD
PATD.
DEC 27th 1864

WOODEN BOOT JACK 199

WOODEN BOOT JACK: Front and rear views of a wooden boot jack used by a Federal soldier. (The wooden canteen is used as a prop only for photographing purposes.) **Markings:** (on reverse side of boot jack) U.S.A.
W W
These letters are crudely carved in the wood. [KEN MATTERN; Wayne, Pennsylvania]

200 WRITING KIT

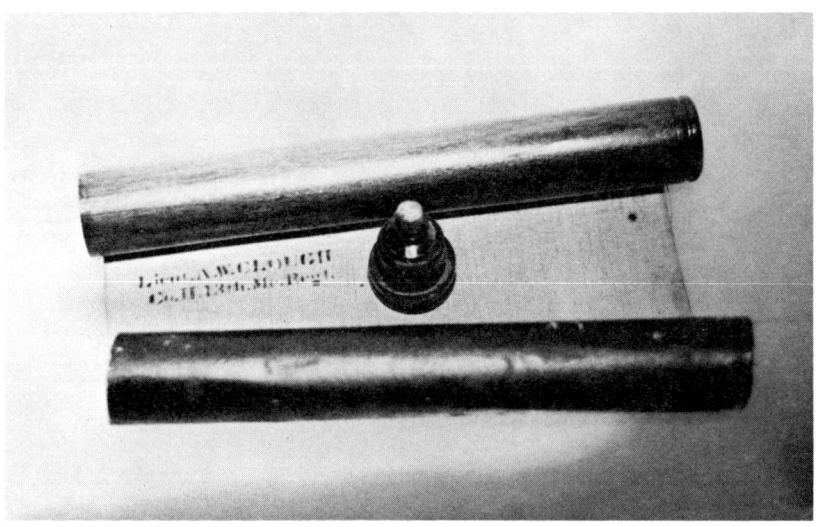

WRITING KIT: Very attractive writing kit; 1 foot long with a diameter of 1⅝ inches. The cylinder is made of hard wood protected by a water-proofed cover. One end of the cylinder unscrews; this end contains a glass inkwell as shown in the photograph. A pen is included in the kit. **Markings:** (on the cover) PATENT APPLIED FOR.

Also stencilled on the inside of the cover is: LIEUT. A. W. CLOUGH
  Co. H. 13th ME REGT

The 13th Maine Infantry served in the 19th Army Corps and lost a total of 195 during battle, disease, in prison, etc.

BIBLIOGRAPHY

In addition to the bibliographies found in Volumes I and II, the following specialized studies are recommended to the reader and collector.

ALBERT, ALPHAEUS H.
Buttons of the Confederacy. Hightstown, N.J. 1963.

Record of American Uniform and Historical Buttons, 1775-1968. Bayertown, Penn. 1969.

[ANONYMOUS]
Civil War Maps in the National Archives. Washington, D.C. 1964.

CAMPBELL, J. DUNCAN AND EDGAR M. HOWELL
American Military Insignia 1800-1851. Washington, D.C. 1963.

COGGINS, JACK
Arms and Equipment of the Civil War. New York, N.Y. 1962.

COLE, M. H.
A Collection of U.S. Military Knives, 1861-1968. Birmingham, Alabama 1968.

CORBITT, D. L. AND ELIZABETH W. WILBORN
Civil War Pictures. Raleigh, North Carolina 1964.

DAVIS, ROLLIN V., JR.
U.S. Sword Bayonets 1847-1865. n.p. 1962.

DONNELLY, RALPH W.
The History of the Confederate States Marine Corps. New Bern, North Carolina 1976.

EDWARDS, WILLIAM B.
Civil War Guns. Harrisburg, Pennsylvania 1962.

GAVIN, WILLIAM G.
Accoutrement Plates North and South 1861-1865. 2nd Edition. York, Pennsylvania 1975.

HARDEN, ALBERT N., JR.
The American Bayonet. Philadelphia, Pennsylvania 1964.

[HARWELL, RICHARD]
Uniform and Dress of the Army and Navy of the Confederate States of America. Philadelphia, Pennsylvania 1960.

HOWELL, EDGAR M. AND DONALD E. KLOSTER
United States Army Headgear to 1854. Washington, D.C. 1969.

HOWELL, EDGAR M.
United States Army Headgear 1855-1902. Washington, D.C. 1975.

KEENER, WILLIAM G.
Bowie Knives. n.p. 1962.

BIBLIOGRAPHY

KERKSIS, SYDNEY C. AND THOMAS S. DICKEY
Field Artillery Projectiles of the Civil War 1861-1865. Atlanta, Georgia 1968.

Heavy Artillery Projectiles of the Civil War 1861-1865. Kennesaw, Georgia 1972.

KERKSIS, SYDNEY C.
Plates and Buckles of the American Military 1795-1874. Kennesaw, Georgia 1974.

LEWIS, WAVERLY P.
U.S. Military Headgear 1770-1880. n.p. 1960.

LORD, FRANCIS A.
Civil War Collector's Encyclopedia. Vol. I Harrisburg, Pennsylvania 1963; Vol. II West Columbia, South Carolina, 1975.

Civil War Sutlers and Their Wares. New York, N.Y. 1969.

Uniforms of the Civil War. New York, N.Y. 1970.

McKEE, W. REID AND M. E. MASON, JR.
Civil War Projectiles. n.p. 1966.

MILHOLLEN, HIRST D. AND DONALD H. MUGRIDGE
Civil War Photographs 1861-1865. Washington, D.C. 1961.

PHILLIPS, STANLEY S.
Bullets Used in the Civil War 1861-1865. Laurel, Maryland 1971.

Excavated Artifacts from Battlefields and Campsites of the Civil War 1861-1865. Ann Arbor, Michigan 1974.

REILLY, ROBERT M.
United States Military Small Arms 1816-1865. Baton Rouge, La. 1970.

RIPLEY, WARREN
Artillery and Ammunition of the Civil War. New York, N.Y. 1970.

STEPHENSON, RICHARD W.
Civil War Maps. Washington, D.C. 1961.

TODD, FREDERICK P.
American Military Equipage 1851-1872 (Vol. 1). Providence, R.I. 1974.

WEBSTER, DONALD B., JR.
American Socket Bayonets 1717-1873. Ottawa, Ontario 1964.

INDEX

	Page
Adjutant's Knapsack (C.S.)	1-2
Alabama Cutlass	3
Anderson Troop Identification Disc	4
Artillery Bridle	5
Artillery Gun Sights	6
Axe Heads	7
Axe Sheaths	9
Barracks Lamps	10-11
Barracks Match Boxes	12
Battlefield Musical Instruments Items	13
Bayonet Scabbard Tips	15
Belaying Pins	15
Binoculars	16-17
Blacking for Shoes and Boots	18
Box Clamp	19
Branding Iron (U.S.)	21
"Break-away" Stirrups and Spur	22
Camp Chair	23-25
Camp Chest	26
Carbine Ammunition Box	27
Carved Toy Cannon	28
Cavalry Bell	29-30
Cavalry Bugle	31
Cavalry Horse Brush	32
Cavalry Tar Bucket	33
Cavalryman's Wallet	34
Chain for Whiffle Tree	36
Cheveaux-de-Frise	36
Cleaning Material	37
Climbing Iron (C.S. Telegrapher)	38
Coat Hook for Barracks	38

INDEX

	Page
Confederate Bowie Knives	39-40
Confederate Cannon Sights	41-42
Confederate Canteens	43
Confederate Cap Box	46
Confederate Flag	47
Confederate Coffee Pot	48
Confederate Pistol	48
Confederate Sabers & Swords	49
Confederate Sharps Bullet Mold	50
Confederate Souvenirs	51-52
Convalescent Camp	53-58
Crows-foot	59
Cumberland Pass Box	60
Daguerreotype (Circular)	61
Dividers	61
Drum Beaters	62
Drum Major's Baton	63
Enfield Bayonet Scabbard	64-65
Fan	66
Federal Shoulder Straps	67-69
Field Candle Holder	70
Field Desk	71-72
Field Signal Lantern	73
Fifes	74
Fishing Sinker	75
Flare (Signal?)	75
Fleam	76
Footbath	77
Frog for Sword Bayonet	77
Fuze Wrenches	78
Gloves and Gauntlets	79
Grater (Potato)	80

INDEX

	Page
Gun Tools	80-82
Handkerchief	83
Harmonica	83
Hatchet Heads	84
Henry Cartridge Box	85-86
Horseshoes	87
Horseshoe (Mud or Snow?)	88
Hospital Bullets	88
Hospital Department Bottles	89
Hospital Flag	90-91
Identification Locket	92
Inspector's Punch	92
Insurance Watch Fob	93
Ivory Pocket Diary	94
Kentucky Kettle	95
Knapsacks	96-97
Leggings	98
Lithograph	99
Map Reader	100
Massachusetts Horn	100
Medical Flasks	101
Mess Kits	102-4
Militia Belt	105
Militia Buckles	105-9
Militia Cartridge Boxes	110-13
Militia Insignia	114-15
Musket Box	116-17
Naval Cannon Lock	118
Naval Cap	119
Naval Mess Knife	120
Naval Shrapnel Fuze Box	121
Naval Signal Light	122

INDEX

	Page
Needlework	123
New Hampshire Drum	124
New York Soldier's Blanket	125
Nosebag	126
Nutcracker	127
Officer's Housewife	128
Oil Can	129
Padlocks	130-1
Painting	132
Pall Bearer's Badge	133
Paper Holder	134-5
Parapet Bayonet	136
Pendulum Hausse	137
Percussion Cap Armlet	138
Percussion Caps & Loaders	139
Pewter Cartridge Box Liner	140
Pictures	141-53
Pills	154
Pinfire Ammunition	155
Porthole	156
Poster	157
Powder Cans	158
Projectiles	159
Railroad Items	160-1
Raincoat	162
Red Tape	163
Religious Medal	163
Revolver	164
Rifles and Muskets	165-6
Saber Box	167
Saddle Cloth	168

INDEX

	Page
Sash	169
Secretary	170-1
Sharpshooter's Glasses	172
Shawl	172
Shelter Half	173
Shot Ladle	174-5
Shoulder Knots	176
Souvenirs	177-9
Spigots	180
Spurs	180
State Documents	181-3
Stretcher	184
Suspenders	185
Tassel for Hospital Patient	186
Telegraph Key	186
Tent Rope Tighteners	187
Toilet Articles	187-189
Tompion Star	189
Tompions	190
Tooth Extractor	191
Tow Hook	191
Veteran Reserve Corps Belt	192
Wagon Wrench	192
War Logs	193-5
Water Filter Canteens	196-7
Wedges	198
Whistle	198
Wick Cutter	198
Wooden Boot Jack	199
Writing Kit	200